The Green Tracksuit

The Green Tracksuit

Peter Gordon Elliot

Published by www.lulu.com

© Copyright Peter Gordon Elliot 2017
Cover designed by artist Colin Brown. www.colinbrown.eu

THE GREEN TRACKSUIT

All rights reserved.

The right of Peter Gordon Elliot to be identified as the author of this work has been asserted in accordance with the Copyright, Designs and Patents Act 1988.

No part of this publication may be reproduced, stored in a retrieval system, or transmitted, in any form or by any means, electronic, mechanical, photocopying, recording or otherwise, nor translated into a machine language, without the written permission of the publisher.

Condition of sale

This book is sold subject to the condition that it shall not, by way of trade or otherwise, be lent, re-sold, hired out or otherwise circulated in any form of binding or cover other than that in which it is published and without a similar condition including this condition being imposed on the subsequent purchaser.

ISBN 978-0-244-94184-0

Book formatted by www.bookformatting.co.uk

Contents

TRACKSUIT 1
THE BIRCHES 8
SIBLINGS 15
DAD & MUM 22
PART ONE 29
PART TWO 36
SNOW 45
THE ALIENS ARE COMING 52
BABYSITTER 60
SHARN 69
G & G 79
THE CURSE 86
FLOATY MAN 96
SUMMERS END 110
TODAY 2017: THE BIRCHES. 112

This is based on a true story. Some of the names and identifying details have been changed to protect the privacy of individuals involved and to ensure their continued safety, but it's also there to protect YOU, anyone who's been told this story wants to go there and see for themselves. I was there and saw, and I moved away a soon as I could after that, I've been running ever since. Stay away from the dark wood.

Follow me on Facebook:

https://m.facebook.com/The-Green-Tracksuit-479496212421943/

TRACKSUIT

Lying washed and neatly folded on my bed, three quarters of the way down my Hong Kong Phooey duvet cover, was my green tracksuit, zipped up with the collar down. I preferred the collar up, but Mum insisted on pressing it down.

It didn't fit anymore. I had worn it that entire summer. I had grown and yes, Mum had probably shrunk it too. But, there it was, my armour. The green had faded and it had a few stains that were never going to come out. The leg was torn and there was a patch on the left knee. Only one of the legs had the elasticated bottom anymore: the other one had given up the ghost- which meant you looked like you were permanently going cycling. Nevertheless, this one hundred percent polyester Adidas tracksuit, with triple white stripes, (well, mostly white), in green, had saved me.

It had been this innocent piece of clothing that had protected me that summer, of that I'm sure. The summer was over, and it was time to put it away. I picked it up, smelt it one last time, (still the distant smell of shite on it) and placed it on the top shelf of my wardrobe. I closed the doors and sat on the bed. There was also a bag on my bed. I hadn't noticed it before for saying goodbye to my beloved tracksuit. I opened it and looked inside. There was a new Adidas tracksuit in red. I pulled it out and looked at it. I sat with it on my lap just staring at it for a bit, Life would go on, red might work. I picked it up and put it next to my old green one in the wardrobe.

I wasn't ready to wear it yet. The green one was barely cold. I would keep the this one, just in case…just in case he came back.

As I prepare to celebrate my fiftieth year on this planet, I thought it was time to tell the story. I still can't explain the events of that day, but what I saw was real, and forty years on it continues to haunt my thoughts.

He is still out there, lurking in the shadows, waiting, for me and for you.

So...if you do hear footsteps behind you, late at night, clonking on the road, you will know he has come for YOU. It's not a mistake.

It was nineteen seventy-six. Scotland was having its hottest summer on record, the hottest summer in five hundred and fifty years to be precise. Temperatures remained in the eighties every day for the entire month of August: still a record, I think. This was the year of Dancing Queen, Raleigh Choppers and Space Hoppers. Although If Space Hoppers were to be believed to be some sort of space travelling device, life in space was going to be slow, then.

The average wage was seventy-two pounds a week, petrol was seventy-seven pence a gallon and a loaf of bread was nineteen pence. Pavements were cracking under the heat and we had a hose-pipe ban of all things- hard to believe in Scotland, I know. Recently, nineteen seventy-six was voted the best summer to be a child in Scotland, if that's a thing? It certainly was for me and my brother James.

I was nine and he was thirteen and we were on eight weeks' school holidays. This would be my summer like no other. There were sunny days like we had never seen before or are likely to again. Every day was a sunny day. I would start the summer as a boy and finish it still a boy; but I had changed. The summer had changed me: I was a lot braver and yet a lot more scared. The events of that summer would live long in my memory and have a profound effect on my life. This would be the summer I would never forget.

Stretch Armstrong was the must-have toy. He was a rubber man you could stretch as much as you wanted and he would always return to his original size. It became a challenge to see if you could break him. Looking back, stretching a rubber man wearing only a small pair of black pants seems a little bit odd now. But, it was the best-selling toy that Christmas, so odd as it may seem, everyone was pulling this rubber man: if everyone was pulling him, it must be okay? Great fun until we broke him. Although I do feel a bit dirty about it now.

When we weren't pulling a rubber man, we could be found trying to kill ourselves on a Pogo Stick, the next latest craze. You would have been safer giving your child a loaded gun. These were lethal, and Accident and Emergency must have had a ten-fold increase due to them. Mainly caused by Grandparents trying to be cool and hip, look at me, look how high Granny can go kids, usually breaking their hip, Mum I think Grannie might be dead, WHAT where is she? Up there. We stopped using ours, as we were keen to see out teenage years.

In Inverness, Eden Court Theatre opened its doors to the public, bringing much needed music and culture to the Highlands. It became a place I would frequent regularly in years to come with my parents. A theatre visit was a special trip. I remember protesting greatly on being told I was being taken to a New Seekers concert, and then being completely blown away by the music. As I sat and watched the guitars sparkling in the lights I was totally captivated. That happened a lot to me. It was less enjoyable when you were dragged along to the Panto, or to Mice on the Moon, when you were eighteen and all your friends were out drinking! Oh no its not ! Yes it bloody is !

Renee Macrae went missing: one of the few times I remember Dad checking the outbuildings. The Police had asked everyone to do this in an appeal to find her. A burned-out car was all they ever found, and to this day, it remains one of the great mysteries of the Highlands.

Harold Wilson was Prime Minister, and Nuclear Engineer and Peanut Farmer Jimmy Carter won the American Presidency. I often wondered if he had been a Peanut Farmer first and then thought; Bugger this, I'm off to be a Nuclear Engineer. Can you imagine the job interview?

'Any previous experience, Mr Carter?'

THE GREEN TRACKSUIT

'Well, yes. I used to grow peanuts actually.'
'Perfect. Can you start on Monday?'

Larry Mullen, a fourteen-year-old Irish schoolboy, pinned a note on the school notice board, looking for band members. That band would become the legendary U2.

And Romanian gymnast Nadia Comaneci scored the first perfect ten, seven of them, in fact, at that summer's Olympics.

Oh, and a small company called Apple started trading. That's never going to work! Who's going to buy a half-eaten apple?

Charlie's Angels, The Dukes of Hazzard and The Six Million Dollar Man were the must-watch TV shows. Saturday mornings were devoted to Swap Shop, obviously. We only had three channels, which seemed to be more than enough, and they were all watched on our one television, which sat in the front room. The family would sit together and watch, although once I saw a very naked lady on the television, and Mum and Dad sent me to bed immediately. Rightly so, I was only nine and naked ladies were scary. If I'm honest, they still are a bit, although my parents aren't generally with me when I've seen them since.

I grew up on a wee croft north of Inverness, in a tiny hamlet. It was about one mile long and everyone knew everyone else. Most people knew what you were having for breakfast before you had eaten it. Doors were rarely locked, keys were left in cars, and the milkman's money was left in an envelope in a makeshift box at the bottom of the road, the box was painted bright yellow, I don't know why must have had some leftover paint, nothing ever matched in the country. Although I don't remember us painting something yellow to have had the left-over paint.

On Thursdays, the Bon Accord lorry would leave a crate of bottles with every colour of the rainbow in lemonade, cue much joy and burping and maybe a little bit of farting, that's a lot of gas for a nine-year-old boy. It would rarely last more than two days and then you had a five day wait until your next fix. A van would appear at the bottom of our road on a Monday. It was supposed to be a grocer's van selling bread and vegetables, but all I ever saw was sweets.

TRACKSUIT

The seventies was a good era for sweets. We had Texans, Star Bars, Dib Dabs and Spangles. Cola was my favourite Spangle. James nearly choked on one once: killed by a Spangle, now that's a way to go! We even had sweets that looked like cigarettes: you don't see many of them now. Despite the fact there were a lot of good quality sweets back then, we didn't get them very often and they were a treat when we did. With the nearest shop being miles away, you couldn't nip out for a 10p mix. We never had sweets in the house, otherwise I would have eaten them all, followed by a bottle of lime cola "tangy"nice.

I think Mr Sweet Van had realised early on that there was more money to be made in confectionary than in bread and potatoes. He was the only mobile sweet van around, so he had the market cornered and came fully laden, with the finest sweets in the land, well, in Inverness-shire. We would spend our pocket money there, maybe twenty pence, and we used to take great delight in asking the man how much his halfpenny chews were. Twenty pence buys a LOT of halfpenny chews, forty-three to be exact.

The hamlet had about fifteen houses and crofts scattered in amongst woods and forests. There was a large disused quarry: a massive hole in a hillside that looked like something had taken an enormous bite out of the earth. The quarry was just at the bottom of the road to our house, and this would be an amazing playground for us. Much fun would be had there, and much danger too.

There was a single-track road that weaved its way through the landscape and then looped back onto the main road North from Inverness.

Crime was unheard of here, although on reflection some of the clothing choices would today, be a lockable-up offence. It was the country after all, and the seventies, so anything went. The fashion was the brighter the better. Country fashion consisted of hand-me-downs, with no regard for the sex of the previous owner. And there was always the belief that nobody would see you, so it didn't matter. Anyway, if they did, they'd be wearing a similarly bizarre outfit, so they would be in no position to comment on yours. When you are nine years old and trying to cut your mustard in the world, it really did matter! Well, it did to me! And people did see you. Well the cows did.

This was a quiet place, you had to make your own entertainment, and that applied to the adults as well, with lots of socialising and parties. Jock, the local drunk, was regularly found face down in a ditch on a Saturday morning having fallen short of his final destination. Every time Mum would think he was dead but he always got up after a prodding and staggered off. I think he is dead now. Or he's a hundred and four. Which is unlikely given the amount of alcohol he could put away, he generally didn't get invited to many of the parties, cos he would drink everything.

There were the usual neighbourly disputes over who owned what, but people were generally friendly. There were the odd one or two who were of a grumpy disposition, some things never change. There weren't a lot of people living here, but those who did were generally good people who understood the land and the ways of the country.

If you had a problem, or needed a hand, you went to your neighbours for help with practical problems like the tractors not starting, or the cows got out. There would have been no point in going to them saying 'I'm feeling a bit sad' or 'what's that love all about, then?' It wasn't that kind of help. Even if it wasn't your neighbour, you would always help, because that's what you do. Certainly, in the country it is. Hello Archie are you free for a quick chat about love? Tractors? No not tractor love Archie, love? No

That's what makes the country work: people, community, kindness, being part of something greater than yourself. I wonder how many people today could go to their neighbours and ask them to help fix the Hen House? How many doors would even be opened? They'd all have to be unlocked first. And that's assuming you even know your neighbours. Things have changed.

Our local school, Bogbain Primary School, was two miles away, and you walked to and from school. Yes, that's right, you walked, until you were proficient on a bike. That's if you had the luxury of a bike. Bogbain was a very small school, with one teacher: Mrs

Urquhart. The class size varied from seven pupils at one point, when Lynn (Sister) attended, to about thirty when I was there. The school day started with us all singing hymns around the piano, and if you misbehaved you got the slipper.

On my first day, I got the slipper. I was five and had been given Plasticine to play with. Primaries one to seven were all taught in the one room. I had used my Plasticine to manufacture a small rectangular shape like a rubber. Eraser is the modern term, always a rubber to me. When the girl next to me asked if she could borrow said rubber, I happily gave her my Plasticine one. Obviously, it didn't work and made a big mark on her book. Sucker!

Turns out, she was the teacher's daughter, and a snitch. I was sent to the cloakroom to get the slipper and was spanked on the bottom with it, *on my first day!* I still remember it now. But I've never made a rubber out of Plasticine since, so it must have had the desired effect.

In the afternoon, you were given milk, long life UHT milk, which was horrible, but which helped to wash down the equally horrible school dinners. There really are no words to adequately describe seventies school dinners. You had to be there to truly experience the horror of cooking on a large scale. And of course, the Wrath of the Dinner Ladies when you didn't eat it all up. More semolina Peter? Can I pass scary, overweight lady?

THE BIRCHES

Our house, The Birches, sat on top of a hill, beneath a larger hill, separated by a large plantation of perfectly uniform fir trees, all about twelve feet high, like soldiers standing to attention on the hillside. It was called The Birches due to the amount of Birch trees growing in the surrounding woods. From the houses' elevated position, you could see for miles, all the way to the Cromarty Firth some miles away. The views were amazing and the surrounding countryside was untouched. It felt like we were the first people to explore it, like pioneers setting foot in to a new land, and maybe we were. Land ahoy, bring me my telescope?

The house was a few miles north of Inverness and about three miles from the local village, but it was isolated and we felt very remote. You could spend ages there and not see or hear anyone for days, although with Dad and Mum's social calendar, that was rare. People were always popping in, bringing things, anything from a side of beef, to hay for the horses. Alternatively, they were collecting things: raspberries, wine, more raspberries, maybe a hen, yellow paint.

More than often they would just come for a cup of tea and a chat. The Seventies was a sociable time, you didn't need an invite, you just turned up. The cups of tea would regularly turn in to drams, and the night would be lost in laughter, and roaring fires. I loved the fact people were always popping in. It made life so much more interesting, and in later years, they would bring attractive daughters, which didn't go unnoticed. It was nice to see Dad and Mum so happy and clearly popular.

It had always been a dream of Dads to own a croft. He loved the countryside and everything that went with it. When he unexpectedly inherited some money from a distant Uncle, Uncle Bill, his dream could finally become a reality. Up until this point they had stayed in a house in Inverness, which they had liked, but Dad always had a longing for some land, where he could keep some animals and play at farming.

I would recommend playing at farming. It's much more fun when your livelihood doesn't actually depend on you being any good at it. We were good at it all the same, but Dad was wise enough to know there wasn't a lot of money in crofting. Playing at farming was bloody great fun though. Let's buy a tractor and plough the fields and see what we can grow! Watching stuff grow is fantastic fun. As is running about in tractors, well, one tractor with dodgy brakes. We'd load trailers up with bales of hay, that we had grown, then feed them to our horses. There was something quite satisfying about it all.

Dad had a tough childhood, losing his mum and his sister when he was just a little boy. Single dads were unheard of in those days and they didn't stay single for long. When his dad did remarry, his Stepmother proved to be of the wicked variety, like in the fairy tales. I think my dad was treated badly by her. She had two children of her own so they were her priority. Dad was pretty much ignored during his childhood, and while his two other siblings wanted for nothing, my dad was given very little.

Sadly, that continued for the duration of his parent's life. Granny's children were always invited for Christmas, and would have regular holidays with them in Rockhaven. We were never invited, and the one Christmas we were, we were made to stay in a hotel. They had the room of course, but lacked the hospitality. Even when his Dad died, he was left nothing, apart from a few bits of Bric-a-Brac. When Granny died, everything was left to her children. He could have contested his father's will, as he was the only blood relative, but that wasn't Dad's style. He would make his own way in the world, despite his poor upbringing.

I heard stories that my Aunts would recount of Dad being sent to stay with them for the Summer, arriving in old tattered clothes full of holes. They would buy him new clothes and send him home at the end of his stay. He would arrive back the following year in the same clothes he had been sent away in. His father had a good job so it wasn't for the lack of money, maybe it was a lack of compassion from his stepmother. Shame that such a kind man had such a difficult start in life.

I never heard Dad talk about his childhood, but when his father died I did see him cry. I'm not sure if that was with relief or if he was just overwhelmed with disappointment. It's a terrible thing to see your dad cry. That was the only time I ever did, thank God. His unhappy childhood certainly didn't get him down. You'd have to look long and hard to find a happier, kinder man. He had every reason to be sad about life, but was quite the opposite. He was determined to have a happy full life. He went out of his way to ensure that we felt loved, and had the best childhood we possibly could. We did, and I know everyone says it, but he was the best dad.

Someone once said to me, as children we are genetically made up of fifty percent of each of our parents. I would be very proud to be half the man my father was. So, I like to think that Uncle Bill had thought time to give Dad a break and give him a helping hand. I always got the impression that the inheritance had come as a surprise to Dad. It had been a substantial amount of money. Dad always spoke very fondly of Uncle Bill, and without him we would never have been able to buy The Birches, and experience that amazing place. We definitely owe him a debt of gratitude. I never met him, but I'm sure I would have liked him.

In nineteen sixty-six, Dad bought The Birches: A Croft of about 80 acres. We had half a dozen fields and the rest was woodland. The house had two rooms upstairs and two downstairs. It was small for our needs and I had not yet arrived in to the world, but over the next ten years Dad set about extending the house.

Growing up in the Seventies was a far cry from the cotton wool society we live in today. People were much more relaxed about things. They didn't live in constant fear for their children's lives.

THE BIRCHES

Me, 1967.

If it hadn't been invented you made your own. That's probably why I'm pictured here in a chicken run.

'LET ME OUT! Has anyone patented this idea, cos I really can't get out? We could be on to something here...

Your parents had lives of their own and a social life, you fitted around them. Yes, you were loved and wanted for very little- although a Chopper would have been nice..., But they weren't running us to Tae Kwan Do, or Ballet every night of the week, in the hope we would be representing our country at the next Olympics, satisfying some unfulfilled dream they had. No, it wasn't like that; they were making their own way in the world, making memories of their own, and rightly so. I might have been good at Ballet, well we will never know now.

Children are important, of course they are, but it shouldn't take over your life. It is, after all, your life as well. So, we were regularly left to our own devices. We were cared for, but we had a lot more freedom than today's children. Maybe our parents were naive, but bad things rarely happened, and when they did they were generally tragic accidents.

I can barely remember a time when we weren't building something. There were extensions on both ends of the house, connecting porch to an old barn that was converted in to a big room for entertaining. It had a wood burning stove, piano, book cases, open rafters and a wooden floor. It would forever be known as the Big Room. A Conservatory was added onto the front of the house, as were numerous outbuildings, garages, woodsheds, hen houses… Dad even built stables. You name it, we were probably building it. The early years of my life, there was constant construction going on.

The field directly in front of the house had been planted in fruit and vegetables. We had rows of raspberry bushes; twelve in total running the full length of the field. We had so many rasps we were giving them away. People would come and pick their own and we still had freezers full of them. We had pretty much every type of fruit that you could grow in Scotland; gooseberries, strawberries, blackcurrants, redcurrants, potatoes, carrots, and artichokes. It was the Seventies and self-sufficiency was the thing. And we were doing it big time, we were even making our own wine. We were living the good life (apart from the odd exploding fermenting wine cask in the night). A poly-tunnel was erected and fully stocked with much exotic sustenance. We were even growing corn on the cob in Scotland.

I suppose we must have been very healthy. Everything we ate we had pretty much grown ourselves or got given by a neighbour:

no food miles with us. I think I must have been seventeen before I realised that not everybody ate raspberries at least once a day (how strange!). I can only remember us healthy and happy, and rarely ill. It would be some time before I would take a waltz with death. I should have kept eating those bloody raspberries.

The only disadvantage of living on top of a hill was that it was a bugger to cycle up when bike technology was still limited to one gear. It could be done, but I think I had only managed it a couple of times. Generally, you would get to half way and then have to push your bike the rest of the way, due to the fact you were completely knackered. When it snowed, Dad couldn't get the car up the road, and boy could it snow. I remember once it was six weeks before we could get the car up the road. Dad made some very brave attempts, with some very scared children, hurtling sideways in a yellow Volvo 144 saloon, with Dib Dab lollypops hanging out of their mouths. So, when it snowed all the shopping had to be pulled up the road on sledges. It wasn't that far, but it was bloody steep and occasionally you'd see a box of mince pies make a bid for freedom bouncing down the road.

It also had its advantages. We always had a good sledge run, although I think we got banned from that because the road would end up a sheet of ice. And if you weren't careful you'd end up with the mince pies at the bottom of the hill. Still, there was always something to eat before you started your ascent back to the summit. The mince pies were probably out of date anyway, most things were in our house. Never did us any harm, well...apart from my Salmonella food poisoning I got when I was twelve. Which ironically, I had contracted from a dodgy sausage roll in Dufftown, and not at home. Mum breathed a sigh of relief. You would have thought after that, the out of date bargain shelf would be avoided, but I think it made her worse. I worried that she'd start raking through the bins at the back of the Spar next.

'Can't we just have a cake that you don't need a saw to cut it with, please?'

'We can afford food that's in date Mum!'

It didn't stop her, she couldn't resist a bargain. She would take great delight in telling us she had bought six mince pies for thirty-nine pence.

'Yes, but it is Easter, Mum! Can't we have Hot Cross Buns like everyone else?'

'No, you will have to wait till August for them!'

There's no doubt we had a pretty idyllic lifestyle; as much space as we wanted, enough fresh fruit and veg to fill a greengrocer, and a landscape virtually untouched... apart from us chopping down the odd tree or three. Well, you've got to keep the fires burning.

My early memories are filled with fun and laughter, Springs and summers, bows and arrows, raspberries and mince pies, good food and cold winters. You went out when you wanted and you came back at tea time. You had no phone, no bottle of water, no sun block, no skinny latte, no Macdonald's and no way of listening to music outside the house, outside a stereo, outside Eden Court theatre... the pain.

The only music you could listen to was your parents'. They had records. My pocket money didn't stretch that far, and I wasn't prepared to give up the halfpenny chews. So, we were on a musical diet of Barbara Dickson, The New Seekers, Crystal Gale and Shirley Bassey. Not my first choice obviously, but it wasn't without some catchy tunes; Caravan, Don't It Make My Brown Eyes Blue. Classics, at least they were in our house.

Top of The Pops, that changed it all. Music on television. This was a new thing. It used to cause much debate in our house as to who was a girl or a boy. Still they played live in those days, and if you ignored the crazy people wobbling about, although they were quite funny, there were moments. The beats were fast. Elvis had stopped vibrating and disco was getting everyone shaking something. Mainly because of ABBA: they started a nation dancing, seemingly freeing people from any inhibitions they might have had, turning them into liberated, gyrating lunatics. It is quite hard not to dance to ABBA. If you were to retain any self-respect in the playground, Top of The Pops was a must watch. Even the Top of the pops albums were legendary, some girl on the cover in a crochet bikini her granny had made, only in the Seventies.

SIBLINGS

By nineteen seventy-six I was approaching double figures. I am the youngest of three siblings. I suspect my parents were saving the best for last, although it didn't always feel like that. I increasingly seemed to be overlooked for anything that might have been new or fun. My sister Lynn and my brother James were both a few years older than me. Lynn was the eldest, but they both tried to boss me around.

'Good luck with that turnip head!'

THE GREEN TRACKSUIT

They would do everything before I did, drive tractors, shoot guns, use chainsaws, ride the horse along the road. (I wasn't so bothered about the latter, if I'm honest. Horses and I got on, but they are quite high maintenance, and all that having to get it ready to go anywhere crap, bridle, saddle, hats, boots, check just to plod off at two miles an hour. Not for me)

Lynn and James also got clothes that were new, and not forgetting Doris and Horace, the pigs! They had a pig *each*, because they were older! I had wanted a pig, but when they were distributed, I was not on the list for a pig! I had been overlooked by the Pig Fairy yet again. This never happened to Lynn and James, the keepers of the pigs, in their fancy new clothes. No, I was doomed to a life of hand-me-downs, and 'can I borrow your pig, please? I promise to have him back by dark.'

Despite this being the era of flamboyant fashion and style, children's clothes were truly hideous and probably homemade from some wool material that had once been a goat. The ones I got were anyway, and mine were second-hand, sometimes third-hand if they had been Lynn's. Oh God.

All that would change soon with the arrival of my new Adidas Tracksuit with triple white stripes in green. It was the Louis Vuitton of the Highlands, a diamond in the rough. It brought new hope that maybe I was important after all. I don't know where it came from, but it was new, and it was mine, and you didn't get *new* often, and this was nice. I could do something with this. It felt bloody fantastic as well. The first time I put it on, I knew I was home. This polyester stuff was comfy *and* groovy. I bloody loved it, I could do anything in that tracksuit.

The elasticated trouser bottoms were a hard look to pull off, I grant you, but they were undoubtedly handy given my terrain. That summer the tracksuit was never off my back. It was my armour, my invisibility cloak, and in green, did I mention it was *new*?

*'Stand aside, I am complete! We are one and together we were greater than the sum of our two parts, the top **and** the bottom.'*

James, my older brother by four years, didn't have a green tracksuit. He was still rocking the flares, long hair, stripes and wellie boots look. Probably not his choice: you wore what was presented to you, washed and left folded on your bed. You asked no questions, and prayed it hadn't been Lynn's.

James was the engineer, the builder, the inventor of all things, and I was his guinea pig. 'Let's turn this Hoover into a jetpack' he'd say. He would give it a bloody good go though, and I would usually end up electrocuted or strapped onto some lethal invention.

One Christmas we were given roller skates. I say we, but I mean Lynn and James. They were a gift from Auntie Betty and Uncle Bill. What exactly were we supposed to do in the countryside with roller skates? We were surrounded by fields. The roller skates were a disaster.

'I'm off out on my roller skates...ok I'm back...just off to change my clothes, turns out they don't work well on grass...'

It was the same year I woke up to see a Space Hopper at the end of my bed, and I screamed the house down. There was an enormous orange head with a face on it and horns staring at me when I opened my eyes! Most people would be alarmed by that.

Going down our steep road on the roller skates would have been certain suicide, so we did what any self-respecting child would do, and screwed two of them to a bit of wood. We called it a 'skate board'- great fun! That's right, James and I invented the Skateboard, we just didn't know it at the time. Well, it had really been James who invented it, but I was the test pilot. There wasn't much he couldn't build, or make, and to this day he remains the same patient, clever, measured thinker. (Unlike me, I was jumping about like a mad man, flashing my bum at anything that moved. I blame the elasticated waist.)

James was always building something, and always in great detail: model boats, planes, steam engines. trying to turn a lawnmower into a hovercraft. I remember he once made himself a jacket with a sewing machine. A proper jacket, with pockets and a zip and everything- it looked good. Who *does* that? My brother.

We always seemed quite close, I don't remember him ever shooting me. which is what you did in the country: you shot stuff. It's not the done thing now, but back in the seventies, it was like

Call of Duty in the Highlands. Everyone had a gun and everyone knew how to use it. We were all sent to Rifle Club from an early age to learn to shoot and to use a gun safely, which was a great thing to learn. The Highlands may have had a large arsenal of weapons, and the locals could probably have out-gunned a small terrorist cell, but nobody ever shot anyone. Certainly, not deliberately…well, not that often.

No one considered shooting someone over some God they follow and you didn't. Terrorism that's never going to work in the country, really. Someone would shoot you before you were over the gate. What's a suicide bomber going to do in the country anyway? Blow up a herd of cows?

'I'm going to blow up your sheep now, Hamish, in the name of Beauly Parish Church!'.

No, that wasn't going to work.

Someone once released a lion up our way. It wasn't unheard of for circuses to dump unwanted, expensive animals in the middle of nowhere. What's more, the newly brought-in Dangerous Animals Act would see it happen more frequently, and we *were* in the middle of nowhere.

There had been several claimed sightings of said lion, including by our next-door neighbour Kenny who'd spotted it only a few fields away. So, James and I would regularly go out 'lion hunting'.

'Bye mum! We are off out lion hunting.'

'Okay boys, have fun and don't be late for tea. It's not out-of-date tonight!'

We spent a lot of time looking for that lion. Friends would visit, and we'd take their kids out hunting too.

'Tom, you haven't seen our kids anywhere, have you?'

'Oh, don't worry Bill they're out lion hunting with the boys. Saw them heading off earlier with the gun. Dram?'

'Aye, I will, Tom. Lion, you say?'

We never saw it, but it certainly made a walk in the woods a bit more interesting. We crawled about those woods for weeks hoping to bag ourselves a lion. I doubt we would have shot it if we had found it. I'm pretty sure that, unless it was a case of self-defence, we would just have run away. Fast, I suspect. I used to imagine going home if we had, saying *Right Dad, that's the lion shot. I'm off to bed.*

There were rumours of various wild animals on the rampage. We never saw or heard anything, although living in the country you do here some bloody scary sounds at night. I think there were animals going about, occasionally you'd find a footprint you couldn't explain. If they were out there, I think they were more scared of us, or perhaps it was James's fashion sense.

I think we fought a bit, but for two boys living in the country, it made more sense to get on. I did once lock him in the barn and then completely forgot I had done. It was a few hours before I remembered and released him from captivity. He was not happy. But, he did jump out on me in the dark once, when I was half way up the road pushing my bike. There was an opening into where we kept the caravan, in the woods, halfway up the road. You could only see in to the opening when you were level with the entrance. This made escaping from scary men, lions, monsters etc., much more difficult, and you'd be knackered from the steep hill.

Anyway, it had always been a fear of mine, and it had never happened. Until one night when James jumped out at me. Bastard! I could have killed him. It was a definite break in the country code: thou shall not scare family members, everyone else is fair game. That's what gives the Highlands its mystique: fear of someone jumping out and scaring the bejesus out of you.

So, as brothers in the country, we had more space than we knew what to do with, enough to get yourself seriously lost. We spent a lot of time together. It was better if there were two of us. The lion might be full after eating Jamie, and I could get away. The lion stuff was a laugh, Mum and Dad thought we were daft, going lion hunting, and so did I. That was until a couple of years later when a large puma resembling a lioness was caught but a few miles from our house. James could have been dinner after all.

Lynn, my older sister, and the eldest of the children, was not so much into lion hunting. She was into horses, and spent most of her time on her beloved Donald. He was quite big, but still a pony. You would regularly see her going around the field, not going over any of the jumps, just riding around them instead, looking at them for half an hour. Donald had it good.

'Oh well, maybe tomorrow he'll jump,' she'd say. 'He was a bit frisky today, Dad, so I didn't try to jump him.' Donald the horse was many things, but he was never frisky.

Lynn would become an accomplished horse woman in time, and would do gymkhanas and horse riding events, just not today. She didn't venture in to the woods like us, unless she was trying to catch Donald, who was not always as keen as Lynn to play horsey games. You would quite often see her running around the field with a bridle. Sometimes there were tears.

One of Dad's many ventures resulted in stables being built, and Lynn's collection of horses grew to five, if you included Paddy the Donkey. Dad rescued him from the Glue Factory and he spent many a happy year following the horses about where ever they went. He thought he was a horse, and I never had the heart to tell him he was a donkey. Dad was always rescue unwanted animals and you never knew what he would bring home next. Mum would despair, but we thought it was great fun. We would have many pets at The Birches. Dad would regularly turn up with some new animals he had found on his travels.

We had guinea pigs, ferrets, puppies, a donkey, peacocks, ducks, geese, several horses and Morag the Highland cow, she wasn't as friendly as she sounds, more of an angry Ginger. He even once brought home a badger, but it was dead, which made it less playful. Turns out Dad had just brought him home so he could bury him. Dad had found Mr. Badger lying at the side of the road. We gave him a lovely funeral, although he wasn't our best pet.

James and Lynn even had pigs Horace and Doris, who they had raised from piglets. Everyday Lynn would carry a bucket to and from school. On the return journey, it would be full of some of the leftovers from the school dinners. You could have filled a lot of buckets with the leftovers from my school dinners. Some of them were still on the plate untouched, complete with knife and fork. This was dinner for the pigs. I was pig-less as I was not deemed mature enough to have a pig.

'What do you mean, Big Ears? I can be responsible!'

Sometimes I would tie a string on to my Space Hopper and pull him along behind me, pretending he was my Pig but Space Pig just wasn't the same.

Unlike us, the pigs loved the School dinners and were thriving on it. They grew to be enormous, and eventually they went away on their holidays, somewhere in Spain, Dad said. I always thought that would be too hot for a pig, but you live and learn. We ate a lot of pork after that; must have been so we could remember them. They never did come back, must have missed their flight.

On winter nights, the horses had to be taken in to the stables, which could be a bit of a palaver in the dark, slipping about on the snow and ice chasing a donkey who thought he was a horse around a field. I'd be there, freezing my tracksuit off, which I had now hooked up with a Parka Jacket: classic.

Lynn was a good sister and tried to mother us, like big sisters do, but we were having far too much fun.

DAD & MUM

You don't get to choose your parents, otherwise my dad would have been Richard Branson and my mum would have been Beyoncé Knowles.

'The raspberries are just over there... to the left to the left'

Now there's a couple! They'd probably have been crap parents: too much pissing about in planes and Hot Air Balloons, or wandering round the house in eight inch heels and a leotard... although, doesn't sound all bad.

No, you get the parents your given, or more to the point they get you, so mine were very lucky then? I think I was the lucky one.

Dad and Mum were two unique people, both bonkers in their own different ways, which made for brilliant parents. Dad in his tweed suits and red socks and Mum in some two-piece home knit she'd wrestled an old lady for at the Kirkhill Jumble Sale. She was the local District Nurse so she got first dibs, otherwise the next time you saw her she might be pulling your plaster off.... slowly.

I wouldn't have traded them, not even for Richard and Mrs B, at least I don't think so. Peter Branson Knowles, does have a slight ring to it though.

'Dad, can I borrow the plane to go down to the Spar for some Cola Spangles? Or the Balloon?'

'Mum, can I help you with your choreography? Ok, one two three, and trousers down flash your bum two three four'. (In fairness Beyoncé already has that move covered).

No, I was quite happy with Anne and Tom, Mum and Dad. .... Is it too late to change my mind?

Mum and Dad both came from Rockhaven, having met there as

DAD & MUM

teenagers. They got married on the twenty-eighth of January nineteen sixty-one in Banchory, just outside Aberdeen. They would spend the next forty-four years together. That's longer than Nelson Mandela got! They never strayed far from each other's side, and always seemed to be quite in love. Not everybody is.

The eccentric surveyor and the jam making district nurse were clearly meant to be. It was a bit like having Willy Wonka for your Dad and Mary Berry for your Mum. Well, not quite Mary Berry, but berries were involved. Maybe Anne Raspberry? But together they seemed to work, and by all accounts were very happy.

A few years later they moved to Inverness. Dad had been offered a job there working for the Highlands and Islands Development Board, known as the H.I.D.B, in our house. He was a chartered Land Surveyor and had studied Agriculture at University. He was to be a Senior Land surveyor and would be mainly working with the rural community, approving government grants for business to expand or diversify in the countryside.

YES, Farmers!

AYE AYE Tom.

If you wanted to borrow some money from the government to start a business, you had to convince my Dad first.

'I'VE GOT A PIG FOR YOU TOM.'

'Please let it be mine, please let the Pig fairy come.'

I think this was quite a good job. He would in due course be offered the top job for the HIDB, which came with a status, and a fancy social life, and probably a new Volvo, maybe even an Estate. He would decline. He loved travelling round the Highlands meeting people, and making friends. To give all that up for a desk job and a couple of extra vol-au-vents at the Christmas party, that wasn't Dad, although Mum might have been tempted. She liked a vol-au-vent.

Dad was all about people. He talked to everyone regardless of who you were because he just liked interacting with people. I think he thought life was much more fun if you got properly engaged in it. He loved people and boy, people loved him. You instantly knew on being presented with Dad that he was something special. That he might actually bring something of value to your life, he would and you would certainly laugh along the way. I find it hard to write about Dad, no words can really describe him. You had to meet him.

All I know is, he was my Dad, who shouted at me when I lost the hammer. (In fairness, it was about the fourth hammer I had lost; never give me a hammer). He would come downstairs with half his pyjamas on, when I'd had a scary dream about the Cybermen from Dr Who.

All my life Dad was there for me, always understanding, and willing to help solve my latest disaster. Later in life I would have a brain haemorrhage and I was lucky to make it back, with a few marbles intact. Although I wasn't allowed to work for a year. Dad phoned me at nine o clock without fail, to check I was ok, every night for a year.

That's love. That was my Dad.

I say that's love, maybe he just had a lot of time on his hands? But it still makes me cry now, when I think of him, how kind he was to me, how lovely a Dad he was, and all the fun... when I'd lost all those hammers! He was a great man, a proper gentleman, full of kindness, and fun. I'm his son, Peter, so obviously, I'm a bit biased.

Mum was busy most of the time, picking fruit, making jams, chutneys, freezing raspberries, thawing raspberries, bottling wine, hanging about the out of date shelf, and entertaining, lots and lots of that. There were always people round for dinner at the weekends. or large parties, there could be two foot of snow and the guests would still come wandering up our road slipping about on the ice, with their bags of tatties, and homemade cheesecakes. The Birches must have been the place to be. It was always full of people. Always in full swing.

'THERES A BAG O TATTIES AT THE DOOR TOM'.

People would regularly bring stuff and just leave it somewhere bizarre,

'THERES TWO PHEASANTS IN THE CEMENT MIXER TOM'
'See you Friday night'.

You would just find stuff that people had left.

'Dad, why is there a peacock in the garage?'
'Oh yes, Malcom must have dropped it off".

They always seemed embarrassed about bringing you a gift, and would always scurry off before you could say thank you. It was like they didn't want to get caught giving you something.

I once found a ferret in a cardboard box on top of the freezer. Mm, must be for James, I thought, I hadn't ordered a ferret. God knows how long he had been there.

'I'VE LEFT A SPINNING WHEEL FOR ANNE IN THE GARAGE.'

Oh God! now she's going to start making her own wool.

On social occasions, we were regularly summoned to the big room to distribute drinks or strange looking nibbles. There was always a lot of people and each time there seemed to be more. For a brief period of my life, I thought I might have been born into a Cult: turns out it was just the Seventies.

'THERE'S A FRESH SALMON FOR YOU, ANNE.'
'Fresh? I will leave it for a few days then, maybe a week.'

Sometimes we would have to perform, me on the drums and James on guitar, nothing else just us. The drums/guitar combo was an acquired taste, although I think we once did a good *Roxanne*. James had a jumpsuit like the Sting from The Police with zips all over it, in green, and with me in my Parka tracksuit mush up, we definitely had a look. I never understood the jumpsuit but it was green.

The advantage of the drums/guitar combo was that it was loud. I'd get carried away and start knocking stuff over, vases and cymbals, anything and anyone in close proximity was at risk. I'd drop a stick or worse both. I think I once actually hit Dr Ferguson with a drum stick in the face, which wasn't ideal as he was Mum's boss. But I think he quite liked it, and no one else had noticed, probably all still staring at James's Jump-suit. Dr Ferguson and I always got on after that, we always had a knowing look between us, that said, I hit you with a drum stick, in the face.

A lot of our songs just ended up with me playing the kick drum: we were like OMD. (Orchestral Manoeuvres in the Dark, popular minimalist band of the time). Our performances were always quite short and we'd be allowed back to the TV room, much to Dr Ferguson's relief. I'm telling you, he liked it! After years as a Doctor dealing with everyone else's injuries, I think he quite liked getting one of his own. I probably made him a better Doctor.

Mum and Dad were quite the entertainers. I think the wine making had proved a success and it was clearly quite potent given the amount of laughter emanating from the big room. There would be many drunk people staggering off in to the night, with a punnet of raspberries or a ball of wool, occasionally both. We would have plenty of time to perfect our musical interludes.

Mum was busy, generally content, not always happy, but always boiling, poaching, stewing, stuffing something. I found it best not to ask. We were always well fed, although we weren't always sure what it was we were eating. Occasionally it might be off, or out of date. Mum did like a bargain and even if it was out of date, it would be fine. Mince pies in March were a bit dry, but once you ate round the mould there wasn't much left to eat. Anyway; we all turned out fine... apart from James's six toes... on his hand.

Not only was Mum the picker of all things you can fit in a jar, she was also the local District Nurse. And a mud-splattered NHS blue Mini could be heard hurtling up our road, sometimes driven by Mum, sometimes driven by me and James shh. If you had a problem or mostly a bandage, and Mum didn't run you over on the way up your drive, she would come and try and make you better. What she mostly did was talk to her patients, as that seemed to be the best medicine, living in the country.

Her constant exposure to cake, cups of tea and people in a lot of pain, meant her threshold for sympathy was quite high. I came in to the house one day with a large plank attached to my foot. I had stood on it and put a four-inch nail straight through one of my toes- the second largest to be exact- and out the other side of my plimsoles. (Trainers hadn't been invented yet, at least, not in the country.)

And did I get rushed to hospital with flashing lights and a police escort? No. It was pulled off my foot, Mum examined the nail, (not my foot) and declared the nail was not rusty so I would be fine. Did I get any sympathy, biscuits, juice and an ice lolly or offered a pig of my own? No. Mum said now hop along to the hen house and see if there are any eggs, there's a good boy.

I had been partially nailed to the cross, well one leg had, then forced to hop round a hen house. Nowadays you'd be in intensive care for two weeks, while Health and Safety conducted a full investigation, including the hen house, and then shut down the farm. I did get over it, but it was bloody sore. You try it! It hurts, You don't get much sympathy in the country, unless you've been shot, and it's generally a bit too late then.

I hated those bloody hens. I had probably been chasing one of them when I impaled said foot on nail. They do tend to shit on everything. It's best to keep them in a Hen House then at least the shit is contained, but they are not free range if they are not allowed to wander about eating stuff. Only problem with that is getting them back in at night, or Mr Fox would be having his wicked way with them, which resulted in a lot of feathers and a missing hen, and a fat fox.

We went through a lot of hens. Dad could occasionally be seen in the front garden, at dawn half naked, sometimes naked, remonstrating with Mr Fox. He was probably heading home with one of our hens, and Dad would be shouting at him, he would always call him Mr Fox, even when he was telling him to *Fuck off.*

'*Fuck off, Mr Fox!*'

It never seemed to stop him,

They had an understanding; Dad would buy hens, Mr Fox would eat them, then Dad would hurl insults at Mr Fox. It seemed to work.

Mum's patients would generally die. Well, a lot of them would; that was the nature of the business, being a District Nurse. A significant number of them were old, and lonely, so although Mum might not have been doing open heart surgery at the side of the road, her work was valuable and I'm sure she brought much joy to her patients. Did I say joy? I meant jam.

I think it was a pretty hard job at times, and Mum was always quite sad when someone died. You'd see her flying about the roads

THE GREEN TRACKSUIT

in her little Mini, driving flat out, probably still in second gear. The car was a mixture of pills, jam and balls of wool. Wool could only mean one thing: a jumper was coming. You'd just hope you weren't the victim. She used to move to the front of her seat when she was overtaking, because that would make the car go faster. Maybe it did, it used to make me laugh.

This was Dad and Mum's time and they were in their element, The Birches was party central, well rural, and everyone wanted to be there. Everyone was always going on about how good the crack was at Mum and Dad's. I did wonder if they were maybe drug dealers.

'How's the crack with you Peter?'
'I don't know, this is a Sherbet Fountain.'

PART ONE

In modern day terms, the Birches was remote. Our nearest neighbour, was probably a ten-minute walk away, or a five-minute run. Obviously, it would depend on who was doing the running. Mum wasn't going to manage five fields, six fences and a stone dyke in that time. Unless, of course, a loved one needed help; she might have managed it then. You do hear stories of people lifting cars, and finding an inner strength they didn't know they had, to save a loved one. However, Mum's cooker was quite new and she hadn't had any problems with it.

There were the MacLennan's who lived a few fields to the south of us; an old Crofting couple and Kenny, their wild son. He was always drunk and in trouble, much to his parents' disapproval. He was much older than us and this was standard country behaviour, getting drunk. I liked Kenny, he was a maverick like me, and he had seen The Lion. At least, he claimed he had, maybe he was drunk, "look a Lion," that's a sheep Kenny". He was old-school, been here all his days, always friendly and quite happy to help you chase a cow or a sheep, providing they had escaped. I don't suppose if you had knocked on his door and asked if he fancied chasing the cows round the field for a half an hour, he would have been quite so keen. Kenny always looked like he could have been a member of Showaddywaddy. Maybe he was, if so, then he kept it quiet.

The Campbells, stayed at the bottom of our road, just off to the left in a little cottage. I don't think I ever saw the Mum and Dad, but the sons Eddie and Roy were trouble and we would do our best to stay clear of them. They were older, and were not to be crossed. Not nice boys, a bit older than us, so we never really stood a chance. So we did what any self-respecting nine and thirteen year olds would do, and stayed well out of their way. I always assumed that their mum and dad were tied to two chairs in the kitchen with gaffer tape over their mouths.

To the East was a mad man who had moved to the area, built a house and then proceeded to fall out with anyone he could. Jack was an angry man who was always in the market for complaining. Falling out with all your neighbours is not a good idea, especially in the country. He once built a fence to stop people going up and down the old road past his house. This was the old back road, and had been a right of way since the Vikings had used it to march their pigs to market. Well, maybe that's not true, but people used it, you can't just put up a fence to stop people walking past your house, because you fancy it. After all, you built your stupid house there. He had barely finished the offending fence, when he woke up to find it had been chain sawed down in the night. I think it was Kenny. Moral of the story: don't move in to the area and try and upset the applecart: there will be repercussions. They won't always come to your door and tell you, like he took great delight in doing, but you will find out their disapproval even if it is with a chainsaw in the middle of the night. Next time it's your arm, Jack!

To the west through the woods was where Miss Mackenzie stayed, an old woman who lived there alone. She would come to ours through the woods, always in black, to collect her mail that was delivered to our house. A very odd, scary woman; if you put a pointy hat on her you would have the perfect witch. That was all she needed. She wore black crocheted shawls and fingerless lace gloves, long skirt and black lace up boots. She had a pale old weathered wrinkly face, that looked like it had been carved out of a potato, and a mane of grey hair, that would have benefited from a bit of conditioner, and maybe a brush. In fairness, I'm not sure conditioner had been invented yet, but I'm pretty sure a hairbrush had. Her ensemble was topped off with a little black hat "not pointy", well slightly pointy, you would never see her in anything else. You would occasionally see her hobbling through the woods, so you would hide, to avoid being turned in to a frog. She always

PART ONE

knew you were there but she would never look at you. She would always pretend she hadn't seen you.... Ribbet.

Sometimes you would come home from School and she would be there. Mum, always the District Nurse, would have invited her in for a cup of tea, and some out of date cake. She would offer you a sweet, she always had Pan Drops. One would be pulled from her pocket and presented to you, not from a bag but from a small pale, translucent wrinkly hand. It was accepted, but never eaten.

I'm sure she was probably just a harmless old widow who stayed alone in the woods, in the middle of nowhere, with no road to her house only a little path that weaved through the dark woods. She was probably in mourning hence the constant black. But there was something about her, a look in her watery eyes, that didn't say sad. I avoided eye contact with her but on the few occasions our eyes had met, it was like in an instant she knew everything about you, every dark deed was exposed in one flash of those pale washed out eyes she knew, and you knew she knew.

It wasn't just me, there wasn't a child within five miles that would go anywhere near that house, or even the surrounding woods. There was a point in the path to her house where you went from one open bright beech wood in to dark wood where the trees were densely packed. That was the cut-off point you never went beyond there ever. A small gate separated the two woods, and to us it was the gates to hell. Well gate to hell.

Let's face it, it wasn't just the children: the adults stayed clear too. Even the Postie, and country postmen will do and go anywhere to deliver your mail. It's like they were on a quest, they were like terminators they wouldn't stop they just kept going until the mail was delivered. Never mind the two foot of snow and the minus fifteen degrees, the earthquake and the flowing lava, Postie would always deliver, but not to Miss Mackenzie's, not to MAGGIE'S cottage.

Maggie's cottage, everyone knew about Maggie's and everyone stayed well away. It must have been only five hundred yards from our house as the crow flies, but with the woods in between it seemed much further, thank God. We used to ask, would you stay in

THE GREEN TRACKSUIT

Maggie's for one night for a million pounds? No was the answer then, and still is now.

Too many stories of weird things and strange sounds coming from there. Bright flashing lights were seen from the windows when the house didn't have electricity, probably only a paraffin lamp. People said they could see them from miles away, from the main road, best part of a mile away. That's not right or possible. Even the cows in the field in front behaved oddly, unsettled and restless. There were regular reports of people seeing odd things at night up there, or worse hearing strange sounds. The house sat at the edge of the woods on top of a hill with a field in front, mostly surrounded by trees, except for the front which looked on to the field.

From the field to the house was a steep climb and from this elevated position the little cottage, poking out of the woods half way up a hillside could be seen from miles away. There had been a door on the front but it had been removed and blocked up, so the only way in was from the wood side, the dark wood, around the back. No thank you, if you need me I will be at home under the bed, wearing my invisibility cloak and rocking back and forth crying. Thanks, but not for all the tea in China, or all the lemonade on the Bon Accord lorry, not even my body weight in half penny chews. I won't be going there ever thank you, I shall heed all the warnings and reports of scary night time activity, and listen to what the disturbed animals were clearly trying to warn us of. If only we had.

James and I would end up inside this cottage alone, or so we thought. That would be a grave mistake.

Hot hot hot mid-July and no let-up in this unseasonal heatwave, I was getting browner by the minute. This was amazing- on the odd occasion I could even be seen in shorts! The trackie bottoms temporarily dispensed with, still the top though, always one piece worn about my person, just to be sure. Berry picking was in full swing and I think we had negotiated a rate per punnet. Still it was a never-ending sea of fruit, and a constant stream of friends filling anything they could carry with raspberries, usually staying for a drink and that would continue in to the night. This was crazy fruit season. If it wasn't ripe today, it would be by tomorrow, and so on.

PART ONE

We prayed for rain and a day off, but there was no break in sight.

The arrival of new bikes for me and James came as a surprise, certainly for me it did. YES NEW, actually NEW, brand NEW bikes! This was like being given your own car, this was Sheena Easton meets Kim WILDE. For the next five years, this was your wheels, your Starship Enterprise, General Lee, Millennium Falcon, Thunderbird 3. This my friends, was FREEDOM... and these bikes were NEW, shiny NEW.

James on the iconic Chopper, the bike of the Seventies, a commander of the playground, a girl puller. If you had one of these you had respect, and you were clearly going places, usually home for tea. This was a big step up for James, it had gears! Three of them! This was NASA technology, gears on a bike! This was reinventing the wheel, literally. He'd have to rethink the wellie boot look for sure. This was one sweet ride. I just hoped he could pull it off.

And me... on its little sister: The Scrambler. Off to the meadow to pick flowers, and search for fairy dust, just before heading home to make cupcakes and put ribbons in my hair. This had girls bike written all over it, apart from writing on it, saying it was a girl's bike. This wasn't going to bring me kudos in the playground. Yes, girls would flock to it, but only to ask for a shot and say I've got one like that! Damn it, I had been humped again. Being the youngest was a definite disadvantage and now it appears they had wanted a girl instead.

The only way I could pull this look off, was to go all out full heterosexual male. Full tracksuit, Parka and plimsoles with hole still in left foot, from the impalement on a nail. A war wound, where I had been shot by a chicken. Well I'd have to bend the truth a bit, to pull this bike off. No more Mr Nice Guy for me! Trouble was about to ride in to town, on a girl's bike in ORANGE, with one gear. No NASA technology for me.... more like *Jackie.*

With new bikes came new friends. We were popular in the sticks, hot in the hills, sweet on the streets, well...the fields. James was clearly adapting to Chopper life rather well. I, on the other hand, was still full on angry aggressive male on a girl's bike, which

I was now starting to like. This was a great bike: I just couldn't tell anyone that. James had become friends with Peter Easton, one of the coolest kids there was. Peter Easton not to be confused with ME, Peter the great. Whilst we might have shared a first name, we were very different. He was very cool and handsome and I was groovy and a lot more handsome. We were opposites really. He had a pretty cool bike as well, a custom job with cow horn handle bars and no back mudguard- radical!

We were mixing with the big boys now. Peter was a good-looking lad a big mop of black curly hair, black leather jacket, faded jeans and trainers. He had it all. not only that but he could ride his bike on one wheel for miles. I've never seen anything like it, he could go for miles and miles and miles just on one wheel. This was a gift from God. He was the Wheelie King. He is probably still wheeling now, somewhere in Africa raising money for disadvantaged unicyclists or something. Peter was a bit wild. He clearly hadn't spent his days picking raspberries, but we liked it and we liked him. He would become a good friend. No one could touch us now that we had the wheelie King in tow.

No sooner had Peter arrived then he was swiftly followed by Hector, another one of James's acquisitions. This Chopper was really paying off. Hector was a different kettle of fish, quiet, reserved and clever: more of a thinker. A tall, gangly, rather awkward shy boy with short blonde hair. He wasn't our usual type of friend, and I think Hector had few friends, but we all got on in some bizarre way. I think Hector needed this, I got the impression his home life wasn't that great. It wasn't that he ever said anything to that effect. It was more what he didn't say, and sometimes you wouldn't see him for long spells.

Hector was also the one who had found, our favourite phrase, carved in a large beech tree in our woods. He had been climbing it as you do and half way up, he discovered a very intricate carving of a naked lady and next to it the words CHEESY FUD. We didn't know what this meant since it wasn't in our recognised bank of swear words, which we weren't allowed to use. We liked the word Fud, and thought it had a certain ring to it, and *Cheesy Fud* sounded

PART ONE

mysterious, and as we had decided it wasn't a swear word we could use it. From that day forward anything we didn't understand was a Cheesy Fud.

FUD would go on to be a recognised word in the Highlands, or more specifically, 'BEING A FUD' or 'DON'T BE A FUD' and 'YOU 'RE A FUD'. Cheesy Fud never really caught on, but 'You're a fud' for a short while would become a globally phenomenon, and even today, the Elders of the Highlands can still be heard calling someone a fud. But I like to think that in some small way we put FUD on the map. We hadn't invented it, but we had certainly helped in making it popular culture. I'm still not completely sure what it means, and not sure I want to know. I always assumed it was some new type of crisps, that the naked lady was trying to advertise, like Cheesy Puffs.

'Want anything from the shop, Peter?'

'Yeah, can I have a bottle of Tizer and a packet of FUDS please? Extra cheesy, don't forget!'

PART TWO

Now we were four, a Band of Brothers. Well, two of us were brothers. We could be seen on the highways and byways, well mostly the byways, following the Wheelie King like a pack of hungry badgers off in search of honey, or maybe we were just going home for tea.

In numbers came bravery, and we were going everywhere and venturing further and further afield. We were inseparable that Summer. ONWARD WHEELIE KING! We did spend a lot of time looking at the back of Peter Easton's head though. He would be out in front, wheelieing everywhere. You could have taken the front wheel off his bike he didn't need it. James was a strong second, and now he had a Denim Wrangler Jacket, ooooh. In the Seventies in the Highlands this was an aphrodisiac somewhere between Oysters and Creamola Foam you would find Wrangler, GIRLS loved the Wrangler.

Where the bloody hell had he got a jacket like that? My brother had changed since he got that Chopper, I didn't know who he was anymore! He'd never mentioned girls before. I was bloody inundated with them with my girly bike.

'PLEASE, can I have a shot Petra?'
'IT'S PETER!'

Hector was third in line in our band, he had a rubbish bike, but it was still faster than mine. I was always last due to my lack of gears, and occasionally I would stop to pick flowers. The bike would automatically slow down when it saw pretty flowers.

We would spend many of our days hanging out in the old disused quarry. You'd be amazed what you can get up to in an old

PART TWO

quarry, and what you might see there. We had taken over the old dynamite shed as our own. This was a perfect hut with a huge steel door. It was impenetrable and with one tiny window the size of your face. Nobody could get in or out once you had locked the door. It was slightly cramped for four, I grant you, but it was a perfect bolt hole if you needed to hide in a hurry from someone, and we needed to hide a lot.

We could sit in there, well stand, it wasn't that big, and spy on the goings-on in the quarry. You'd see people dumping stuff they shouldn't, and stealing stuff they shouldn't. Once we even saw a car drive in, park behind a pile of gravel and then the car started rocking back and forth, slow at first then faster. When we sneaked up to inspect the strange activity of this mobile washing machine, we were forced to leg it back to the dynamite shed rather quickly. that's far from a washing machine.

We were all slightly traumatized, but not as much as the young couple were, when they saw four rather shocked boys peering through their steamed-up windows. The couple quickly put their clothes back on and left at speed, so maybe it had been a mobile clothes cleaning device after all.

When we weren't in the quarry we were either fishing or in the woods building huts. Fishing was the new cool and everybody was doing it. We would regularly head off to the Fairy Den, a forest walk about three miles away, with a river that ran through it. It was called the Fairy Den because fairies reportedly lived there. I would fit in nicely then, on my bike. (I wonder if there's any Fairy Dust?)

This was the perfect fishing spot. I'm not sure we ever caught anything. I think sometimes we did, but it was an outing for the Wheelie pack and as it was full of walkers and ramblers, we could get up to mischief. We were always hiding from something or someone. We weren't very sociable, first sign of anyone and we were hiding. This was where the green track suit came in to its own. I could blend in with any surroundings; providing they were green, I was invisible to the naked eye. We would become masters of disguise.

The sunny days seemed to go on forever, and you'd arrive home exhausted and usually covered in mud and twigs. We were outside all the time, no computer games for us. You made your own entertainment because nothing had been invented yet, and I'm glad that it hadn't. Although some hair gel would have been nice. My hair was getting long (as was everyone's) and all you could get was Brylcreem, which was greasy, and made your hair look like you worked in a chip shop. Mock chop anyone?

Our numbers had now risen to five, with the arrival of Euan. He had been recruited by me. He was small and of a timid nature. He also had a Grifter: another highly sought-after bike of the time. Great! Euan always looked undernourished, I'm sure he wasn't, but he was very thin. I guess he just hadn't sprouted yet. Despite his small frame, he was a good footballer and he had a full-sized set of football goals in his back garden. He was in. Euan and I would be good friends. Turns out Peter Easton was pretty handy with a ball as well. 'Is there nothing he can't do!? I also had some moves I could bring to the table. James not so much but he had the Chopper and now the Wrangler jacket, so he didn't need to bother.

We would play for hours, but always leaving before it got dark. We were still uncomfortable going up the road at night with the dark wood so close. There had been reports of more strange noises, and no one had seen Mrs. Mackenzie for ages. We had tried to forget about Maggie's, but now it was firmly at the forefront of our minds. We would always be home before dark no matter what: even going up the road at dusk was scary enough. Autumn was on the horizon and soon it would be dark a lot longer and a lot earlier. The safety of the summer sun would soon be gone.

An overly dramatic penalty shootout one night would see me lose track of time at Euan's, and I returned later than I had hoped. I was alone, and despite frantically pedalling the two miles home on my girls' chariot, I reached the bottom of our road to complete darkness. I was exhausted, cycling up was not an option. I would have to push my bike up the road.

The moon was lost in the sky, smothered by the mist, just a faint glimmer of brightness above the trees. It was eerily still. A thin film of misty fog was rolling off the woods, like cigarette smoke, lying

PART TWO

heavy on the grassy verges, punctuating my path. Normally the sound of some animal scampering through the woods could be heard, or the distant sound of a car, but tonight it was completely silent. Nothing but my anxious breath which was becoming faster. Five minutes, maybe four, and I would be inside the house safe and sound. It couldn't have looked creepier than if I had actually been on my way to Castle Dracula.

I was used to the dark though, and had done this hundreds of times so I told myself I would be fine. You learn to rationalize sounds at night in the country. There's generally a logical reason for everything. I tentatively set off knowing that, in a matter of minutes, I would be safe at home. The clicking of my bike chain like a stopwatch timed my progress.

As I left the safety of the main road I was fully embraced by the dark. Slowly, my eyes adjusted and I could see a bit more. I was half way to the corner, then the big hill and home. I was starting to feel a bit calmer…nearly there. Suddenly, I saw something moving in the woods to the left of me. I paused. My senses scanned the air: nothing. It must have been a cow or a deer. I increased my pace. Another few steps and it moved again, at speed this time: a large figure. This was no bloody cow.

It jumped the fence and stopped and stood in the road directly in front of me. I stood motionless hoping it would go, hoping it hadn't seen me. My already racing heart had now reached nuclear proportions. My eyes were transfixed on this figure that was less than twenty feet in front of me.

I gripped my handle bars ready to turn and make a bolt for it. There was something standing in the road and blocking my way and I was not going to hang about to find out why. We both remained motionless: it felt like an eternity. I felt sick, my mouth was dry. The tall, shadowy figure stood directly ahead.

I tensed all my muscles ready to explode and was just about to when it came to me James, up to his old bloody tricks. I laughed and was somewhat relieved.

'You scared the shit out of me you Fud!' I shouted, and started walking towards him. Thank God, what a relief. He also started walking towards me. 'Bastard' James you utter Bastard.

He must have been five feet in front of me when I froze and stopped dead in my tracks. I think my heart stopped. A man with a pointy beard and a long coat emerged from the dark. He was skinny, with a pale face and long boots that clonked on the road. As he walked past me, he slowed down and turned his head and looked straight at me. His deep-set dark eyes never left mine. I was transfixed to the spot. I couldn't move.

As soon as he passed me, the clonking stopped. I turned my head knowing he had stopped, preparing to meet my fate.

He was not there. He had vanished.

I dropped my bike and ran flat out like I'd never ran before. Even when I thought I couldn't run anymore I kept running, and getting faster. I thought my lungs were going to explode. The lights of the house drew closer and closer and I ran straight in to the house and locked the door with both locks as fast as I could.

I lay crouched on the floor behind the door gasping for breath. What the hell had just happened? I hadn't imagined it. Who the fuck was that person, why did he stop in the road, and where the sodding hell had he gone? My leg was bleeding. I must have fallen and my tracksuit was ripped at the knee. I sat there for twenty minutes, motionless. My heart was still racing but at least I could breathe now.

I went through the house to the TV room to where Dad and Mum were. Close to tears, I told them what had happened. Dad immediately went out to look. He returned shortly after having seen nothing but he had recovered my bike. Even James seemed genuinely concerned. Apparently, there had been some Gypsies going about and there had been reports of some thefts from local farms. The next day Dad checked all the sheds and put some padlocks on the garages. I think he even went and told the local Policeman.

Mum and Dad both did their best to convince me I had scared myself, and that the fact I had thought it was James had caught me off guard. They believed that had given me the biggest fright. But I knew this was no opportunist thief hiding in the shadows looking to

PART TWO

steal a hen. This was an overly confident man, bold as brass, quite happy to scare a child half to death, and gloat in the process. That look he gave me, albeit brief, was in slow motion to me. His eyes were enjoying my suffering, deep set small piggy eyes full of glee at my fear. Pure evil; this was no gypsy.

Whoever it was, I had inadvertently called them a FUD. If you do meet the Grim Reaper on the road at night, I wouldn't recommend your best plan of survival is calling him a FUD. I hoped he was a forgiving scary man.

Unfortunately, we would meet again.

The next few days I stayed close to the farm. I was so disappointed that this had happened. I asked myself, what had happened? Had I seen a ghost? I knew it wasn't a gypsy. If you'd seen him, you would know that. He looked like he was from another century, even for the countryside he looked out of place, almost like he had stepped off a ship from the fourteen-hundreds.

My bubble had burst. No more coming home alone in the dark. I should have stayed at Euan's that night. I so wish I had, then I would never have seen that man, with his look that sucked the life out of you, and made me realise that evil was out there and it knew who I was, and where I lived.

James had informed the Wheelie Pack, and they were summoned to the house, well, the barn. Even Peter Easton admitted he would have been scared, Hector and Euan seemed genuinely to be shitting themselves. There was much debate as to what I had seen. James knew and believed everything I said. He knew me, and he had seen me that fateful night. I think Hector and Euan were too scared to contemplate that this had actually happened and that something was out there. They did their best to reassure me, although I think this had shaken us all. We were all home before dark after that.

I moped about the house for a few days, then one day I found my tracksuit washed and folded on my bed. Even the hole in the leg had been repaired, another war wound. I say repaired and it had been, with a perfectly matching patch, but now my pocket had a hole in it. The good Lord repaireth and the good Lord taketh away. I put it on. The trousers were becoming rather short. Either I had grown or mum had shrunk them. Probably the latter: Mum and washing machines were not a match made in Heaven. It was not uncommon to find that some of your clothes had changed colour during the washing process as well. This tracksuit had survived a lot and was still green. It smelt great and it still felt great. It had protected me so far, and it would still. The summer was not over yet, and no scary man could touch me in my armour.

Come Hell or high water (hopefully not Hell), I thought, I'm going to find you, and we will have this out.

The Wheelie Pack thought I was mad and were not as convinced as I was that this was the best way forward. James was onboard. He knew we had to find out who this was or we would forever be looking over our shoulders. Peter Easton agreed: he would punch him. Peter liked punching things and this would give him a goal. I had been unable to move when I saw the man, so this would be interesting. Hector and Euan had packed their cases and were preparing to leave the country. They wanted nothing to do with this. I could understand that, but we needed them, because three of us would not be enough. If I had had the Wheelie Pack with me on that night, things would have been very different. I needed them with me now, and after much persuasion, they agreed. Together we would be strong,

He was only one, and we were fast and cunning and we knew every shortcut and hiding place there was. Operation Scary Man was on.

We scoured the woods for clues, started with where I had first seen him, the woods at the bottom of the road. nothing was found. The fence was high at the point he had jumped it, the ground on the wood side was lower there. We all tried but none of us could clear it, and we were used to jumping fences. He was clearly fit. The bushes where he had vanished were too short to hide someone. People don't just vanish in to thin air, certainly not people of this earth.

Every day we conducted a different search. We examined each local wood in detail, all except the dark wood which lead to

PART TWO

Maggie's. That was still out of bounds, for now.

Euan did find a boot print which was overly large, at the corner of the road, but just one. This was enough for Euan to head home with the excuse of a forgotten family outing. It was strange and it was heading in the direction of the dark wood, but hardly conclusive evidence. Our investigations were giving us nothing and becoming quite boring. The scary man wasn't so scary anymore. Whoever he was, he wasn't around anymore.

Life quickly returned to normal. I even had a few trips up the road at dusk by myself. All was well again.

On an up note, Mr. Fox had clearly got fed up of Dad's naked abuse, and our hen population was thriving. (In my experience, you are more likely to listen to someone who is naked and shouting at you, than someone who is clothed. You're more inclined to look at them certainly, and because of that, you listen to what they are saying.) Mr. Fox hadn't been seen in ages, so obviously, Dad's naked ranting had worked. I might try that next time I'm off to have an argument with Mary at the Spar, because she sold me June's copy of the Look-In (cool popular music magazine) in July.

Where the Hell is July's Look-In, Mary? ...Yes, I'll put my clothes back on... Sorry Mary... just trying something out.

No, naked ranting is not for me. I'll just read Junes' edition twice, and keep my clothes on, thank you.

WHERES MY CLIFF PIN UP MARY? WHERE?

Dad was as delighted with the departure of Mr. Fox as was Mum with the eggs. Baking was in full swing. The party season continued. Well, it was always party season at the Birches, and Dad and Mum knew some characters. There were always many strange tweedy outfits on display, and bizarre hats that might have once been an animal. Men wore shirts that looked like someone had thrown a pan of lentil soup at them. Women wore some very bright vibrant frocks with swirls on them. If you looked at them for too long they would hypnotise you. There was always so much laughter in our house. I did wonder if the laughter was just them looking at each other's hideous outfits.

It was like Mos Eisley Cantina, (the cafe in Star Wars where all the aliens hung out).

Come on, it will be alright, Chewy... I mean James.

Bless them, they seemed to be having a ball, literally and on most nights of the week. Our musical exploits were in high demand and sounding good into the bargain. I'd had a few drum lessons and had learned that less was more. There were certainly fewer breakages, although I think Doctor Fergusson was disappointed, less exciting for him. We were starting to enjoy our performances and would have to be encouraged to stop.

'But...we've got more!'

'One more song.?... Anyone? Dr Ferguson?'

SNOW

Snow is a common occurrence in the Highlands. For the children, it means days off school and endless fun exploring this fantastic new landscape. It's much the same for the Adults, who've worked out that there's no point in trying to get to work if you live in the country, because you just end up not being able to get home.

When there was snow, which was quite often, Dad would just stay at home, as did we. Our School would be closed for sure: the first sign of snow in the country and the schools were closed. It was brilliant fun.

Snow instantly turns everything in to a Winter Theme Park, full of death defying rides. At least, it did for James and me. Fields that had only the day before had been boring undulations in the landscape, were now transformed in to lightning fast toboggan runs and dangerous ski jumps, sledge runs and slippery ice slides. We built them all. James and I could make anything out of snow. We had years of experience of working with this crystallised gold. When the pond at the bottom of the road froze over one year, there were even people curling and ice-skating on it.

Secretly, I think everyone in the country loved snow, and if they didn't they weren't Local. What's not to like about snow? It's AMAZING. Dad loved the Snow nearly as much as we did, and at first sign of it Dad was off to the shops, as he would say "to get supplies" in his latest strange arrangement of clothes. Mary at the Spar was in for a treat. She was probably still getting over my last naked visit.

'Hello Tom, what can I get for you today?'
'Two bottles of lemonade, one bottle of whisky, and all your

THE GREEN TRACKSUIT

bread please, Mary'
'All my bread, Tom?'
'Yes Mary. All of it'
'BYE Tom... Nice wellies, by the way.'

It wasn't uncommon to see Dad in wellies that didn't match, not just different makes, but sometimes completely different colours. He'd wear one black wellie and one green wellie, which I can only describe as brave. In this stroke of genius, he had also doubled his collection of wellies. I think he had once had to put wellies on in a hurry to rescue Mr cow who was making a bid for freedom, and had just put his feet in the first thing that came to hand. That was the Eureka moment, after that the gloves were off, or more to the point, the odd wellies were on.

Dad would return home from the Spar a short time later with twelve loaves of bread. By then the snow had usually stopped and the sun was out now. And we had twelve loaves of bread...

'What's for tea?'
'Bread.'
'Oh...'

I never liked Wellies. They were never very cool and I never connected with them. I know they are practical, but you do look ridiculous in them. You never hear James Bond saying, I'll just get my wellies on. You're woken at two a.m. in the morning by a phone ringing. You answer: it's the British Secret Service.

Can you escort the Princess over the border tonight at speed?
I'll just put my Wellies on then...Princess, you say?

Nobody has ever said *God, you look sexy in wellingtons, darling*, apart from maybe a few Welsh farmers. They don't have a huge range of wellies in Ann Summers, certainly not that I've seen, although it is hard to see through those dark glasses I wear to go there.

'Make love to me! Take me! I want you, stud-muffin!'
'Ok, my love, I'll just get my Wellies. Do you want matching? Or are you ok with odd?'
'GIVE ME ODD, BIG BOY!'
'Right you are.'

SNOW

At the first sign of snow you would get excited. You would be sitting in class at school and as soon as you saw that first flake, you knew that if it kept snowing for the next ten minutes, you would be sent home. The larger the flakes got, the more excited the class would get, and the more nervous the Teachers would get. They didn't want to be stuck with the responsibility of not being able to get children home. James Riddle (not his actual name) stayed at the top of a hill, in the back of Beyond. He was also a serial widdler and there was a constant wet patch on the floor under his desk. Riddle by name, Riddle by nature. He might have been responsible for the classroom smelling like a toilet, but thanks to him we all got sent home early on many occasions. Good old STINKY.

It was a different case for Mum, she had to get out. She was the District Nurse, people depended on her, and in the Winter months they depended on her even more.

Most of her patients were highly addicted to Raspberry Jam, and needed their daily fix. In the seventies, jam was widely available and everybody used this sticky substance. It was highly addictive and widely recognised as a gateway drug. Many users would in time find themselves dabbling with Cake and in extreme cases this would lead to the hard stuff: TABLET. The manufacture of Scottish Tablet had been overlooked in the nineteen seventy-one Misuse of Drugs Act, despite it being highly addictive. And its manufacture was still allowed. Old ladies would regularly have cook ups late into the night in the Highlands. Each had her own secret recipe, the basic ingredients were sugar, condensed milk and butter, but each Granny Pablo Escobar had her own take on it. The Highlands was full of it, and it was widely available.

The Grannies had set up their own clever distribution network using, coffee mornings, jumble sales, and they were even selling it in church under the pretence of funding a new roof. You'd need a lot more than a new roof after this stuff. It was always sold in a clear plastic bag so that you could see your stash, and cost anything from fifty pence to a pound. The making, distribution and pricing was tightly controlled by a cartel called the WRI (Women's Rural Institute). The WRI were a motley crew of middle aged women, wearing polo necks and pearls, standard issue uniform, proficient in anything that was crafty, from patchwork quilts, to knitting and baking. They would even collect old bars of soap that were nearly finished and melt them all down to make one big multi-coloured bar. They were cunning, highly skilled and not to be messed with, or you would find yourself sent to bed early.

I heard a story once of a man who ate a whole bag of tablet. Rumour has it, he talked for three days nonstop. I tried it once but only cos my friends were doing it. It made me very sick and that night I didn't eat my tea.

But Mum was just giving her patients jam because we had so bloody much of it. We had to get rid of it somehow. She was never involved in Tablet making, she always burnt hers.

One Hogmanay, Dad and Mum arranged to have a party: a large one, everyone was invited. Mum had spent weeks baking, stuffing, and poaching, as usual. Dad had been bottling wine, anything he could fill had wine in it. Wine Galore. Even Lynn had been involved in the baking process. This was a two-woman job and this party was a big operation. My parent's friends were big eaters and equally big drinkers. It was the Seventies, there was nothing else to do in the winter, and Hogmanay's were generally quiet, (there's only so much Calum Kennedy you can take). Not this year, the world and his dog were coming. In fact, there probably would be dogs coming. New Year's Eve arrived and the day of the party, we opened the curtains to three feet of snow, and no electricity.

Dad and Mum were gutted, we had enough food to feed Uganda, and enough drink to get Ireland merry. Breakfast was a subdued affair, hardly anyone touched their Horace and Doris (Bacon). Mum looked traumatised. She just sat looking at the Cooker, hoping the light would come on. It didn't and was unlikely to. She would have to use the unreliable Rayburn for her cooking now. She had baked her ass off and for nothing! No one would come now, most of them couldn't find their cars, let alone get out their drive.

If you've never woken up to three feet of snow, it's one of most magical experiences you can ever have. When you open your

SNOW

curtains, expecting the usual winter dullness, and you are confronted with a blinding winter wonderland. It's truly spectacular, it's like going to bed in one world and waking up in another. This snowfall was amazing, all the untidiness of the country had miraculously disappeared over night, covered by a blanket of brilliant white magical snow. When you're a teenager, which I *almost* was, this was the most fantastic thing ever. Snow snow snow! This meant fun, and lots of it.

This was a serious amount of snow. I'd never seen so much in one night. Everything looked like the top of an iced Christmas cake, smooth and untouched, but not for long. The Poly tunnel could hardly be seen, and the snow was making it sag in parts. It looked like the Loch Ness Monster was in our field, (which does exist by the way).

The phone rang all morning with people asking if the party was still on? Dad, always the optimist, was determined it would go ahead and people would come. I thought that was unlikely. We struggled to get out the porch door. The snow was deeper than our wellies. We spent all morning clearing the road so at least there was a path you could walk up. We couldn't even get the car out of the garage let alone down the road.

Half the highlands were without Electricity, and given the weather conditions that wasn't going to change anytime soon. We set about finding every old paraffin lamp, we had or anything that could create light. You keep everything in the country, never knowing when it might come in handy. We found more than we expected and even a box of Church candles, probably a present from one of Mum's patients. The things old people think you might need, and on this occasion, they were right.

Our jobs complete we were released from our chores, and immediately set about building a sledge run from the house to the field. There was so much snow. The rest of the day was spent sledging and skiing. We even built an enormous snow man at the back door to welcome our guests, complete with a large candle covered with a jam jar, illuminating the path just in case anyone came.

THE GREEN TRACKSUIT

By the time, it was dark the house looked amazing all twinkling with flickering candles, and paraffin lamps. The fires were roaring and the house was cosy as anything. The snow just made everything look so beautiful. But would anyone come, could anyone come? The news was advising people to stay home, keep warm, and make no unnecessary journeys.

Clearly though, coming to our party was a necessary journey. Country people never do what they are told. Over a hundred people turned up at ours that night, in various snow-going outfits. They came walking up our road carrying food and candles. Some came on sledges, some even came on skis. It was a sight to behold. There was a pile of jackets the size of a haystack in our front porch.

Kenny MacLennan had put a snow plough on his tractor and cleared the side road so that people could get their cars at least to the bottom of our road. It was the greatest party we would ever have, and went on till dawn, most people stayed up all night drinking. On the stroke of twelve James and I skied down the fields with flaming torches we had manufactured with rags and left-over Paraffin. It looked amazing. Talk about making best of every situation. What a way to see in a new year.

The party had been a huge success. We still had people the next morning wandering about wondering where the hell they were. All Dad and Mums hard work had not gone to waste. The house was a bomb site though. That's the thing about people in the country: if they say they're going to do something they will, and if there is food and drink involved they will definitely will. The party was talked about for many years, and would go down in history, well countryside history.

That same snow fall would see us build a full-size igloo in the front field. *James, do you want to build an Igloo? bugger off I'm sleeping?* It would remain there until April. Even when all the snow had gone we still had an Igloo in our field: classic. We were without electricity for two weeks. We removed the contents of our freezers, meat and endless punnets of you know what, and buried them in the snow. When the electricity came back on we dug them back up and put them back in the freezer. It all seemed to work well.

SNOW

For six weeks, we had to walk up and down the road, carrying everything and anything and slipping and sliding about all over the shop. Best of all, my Primary School remained closed for two weeks-bloody brilliant. It was undoubtedly the most and the best snow I've ever seen in my life. I love snow. Even now I open my curtains every morning in the hope that I might once again be transported back to that magical winter land, yelling 'SNOW! James, SNOW!'

THE ALIENS ARE COMING

The Summer was nearly gone, and a return to School was looming on the horizon. Soon my tracksuit would be dispensed with and replaced by a God-awful school uniform. The Wheelie Pack were still spending all their time together and our new hobby was building huts in the woods. Mainly at ours, as we had the most trees. We had built several huts already, but once it's built, you sit around in it for a bit then it's on to the next one.

James was in his element as chief designer. He strode about the woods like a young Lawrence Llewelyn Bowen, in his Wrangler jacket, flouncing about, pointing at stuff, stroking his long hair. You'd have thought he was Michelangelo creating his latest masterpiece. 'It's just a hut, you TIT!' I reminded him.

Each new hut would be of a more grandiose design. Our latest one was going to be built up in the trees. We had found four trees of similar size in a square shape. This raised elevation would provide us with a great vantage point over the woods. Let the build begin…

Jamie collected National Geographic Magazines. I told you he was weird. This had been his inspiration for the new hut. He presented us with a picture he had found, there was a massive bamboo hut built up in the trees and below eight men who had obviously built it, they had spears, bows and arrows and were completely naked, wait a minute Those guys have obviously just had a massive argument! I'm not sure it works if you're all naked. I think just one person has to be naked. I'm not building a hut in the buff: you've gone too far this time, Llewelyn-Bowen! I wasn't for using a hammer when I was naked. God knows what you could hit! It's bad enough when you hit your thumb with a hammer. And I wasn't going to see Dr Fergusson and try to explain to him how I hit my own willy with a hammer. He already thought I was lunatic.

'How can I help you today, Peter?'

'Well Doctor, I seem to have inadvertently hit my willy with a hammer.'

'That looks sore, Peter.'

'You don't say!'

No, I insisted that we keep our clothes on. Turns out James meant the hut, not the naked labourers. Oh, well where the hells the Bamboo then Donkey Kong?

This construction was even close to the Dark Wood. It was the only place we could find the perfect four trees, but the Dark Wood didn't seem so dark anymore, since we'd given up trying to find Scary man. He'd gone.

We had better things to do, like hitting our willies with hammers (which is not a phrase I thought I would ever use).

We were very busy. This was a big build, even for us. We wandered back and forth through the woods with various materials, tools, wood: anything that might be handy. Well...at least, I did. After a week of being bossed about by 'Adolf' Elliot, (who didn't seem to be doing much, apart from ordering me about, and sending me to get stuff) our hut was completed and the Wheelie Pack could now sit high up in the trees, surveying the surrounding woods. I needed the rest. You had to climb up a rope ladder to get in to it, which could be quite tricky, but that would also help keep most people out. Lynn and Mum weren't going to pop in for a cup of tea, that was for sure. well we didn't have a kettle- an oversight by our great leader, Herr James.

We felt safe up the trees, like Robin and his Merry Men. We were men of the woods, well... boys. We had catapults, bows and arrows and pocket knives; all the things you would never give to your children nowadays. Back then, these were necessities for every boy's daily survival in the country. The Hut even had a large glass window we had borrowed from Dad's workshop.

Stealing his stuff, I mean borrowing it, was common practice. It had only gone wrong a few times when Dad wouldn't be able to find something he needed, and then me or James would have to leg it through the woods to retrieve said item.

'Where's the bloody hammer?'
Oh, I might know where that is...Sorry Dad,
I think I might have temporarily mislaid the hammer again...

I spent a lot of time running. (That's five hammers I've lost now). It was only a matter of time till Roy Castle came to give me my Record Breakers Medal, and I would be put in the Guinness Book of Records, as the World Record holder, for losing the most Hammers. Although I think there is some bloke in Chile who has lost seven.

One evening we had all been invited to the Maclean's; friends of Dad and Mums and regular attenders of our parties. They had children of similar ages to us. Anna was ages with Lynn and liked horses, Philip was ages with James, who was also a keen inventor of all things dangerous, and I was the same age as Karen, who also had a girl's bike. I liked Karen, she was fun and a bit of a Tomboy. We all got on well and visits there were always fun. The evening would usually involve about half an hour of feeling uncomfortable when you first arrived, because of having to talk to adults and not having seen our playmates in a while.

Then after dinner, we would be released and set free to play. They had a big farm and lots of big steadings full of bales of hay and grain stores: a veritable playground. They even had a loch you could swim in and we would often have picnics and go swimming there. All very *Little House on the Prairie*. The loch was always a bit cold for me, and I never felt too comfortable with part nakedness. I'm more of a clothed boy at heart.

The odd summer or two we would be sent to mum's parents in Rockhaven. Grandfather would always insist:

'Get your sark off lad! It's a lovely day' (which is old speak for get your top off)

'No thanks'

'Get your bloody top off lad!'

He would always order James and I around. He had been in the War and you were never really given an option, you were always told. Then you would have to spend the rest of the day wandering around looking like you'd been dipped in flour, just to keep him happy. Yes, I probably have skin cancer now Grandad, thanks to you. It used to piss me off. It wouldn't happen nowadays, now they've invented sunblock.

But this evening at the Maclean's we were all playing outside. Well, all except Anna and Lynn who were probably exchanging horsey photos or old copies of *Look-In*. I quite liked the *Look-In*. *I never said that, ok? Hmm, I hope she got July's edition. I needed that Cliff pin up"*.

We were all on a large pile of hay bales. This was a whole lot of bales and perfect for hide and seek or whatever we were playing when we notice lights in the sky very close to us. Lights, but no noise, a cigar shaped object came in to vision, *what the fud*? Philip ran and got his dad, and our dad appeared outside as well to watch the strangeness. The mums never moved from their drinks. There could be an Alien invasion and they'd still be talking about how they'd boiled a ham in Coca Cola.

'Oh, hello Mr Alien! Come in. Now, how do you poach your salmon on your planet?'

We all stood outside for about fifteen minutes watching these strange objects in the sky. More had appeared now, all large and cigar shaped, with lights but making no sound. This was 1976, long before drones had been invented and these things were massive. They had only just invented the calculator and the radio watch. We knew: we had got them for Christmas. If you gave someone a calculator for Christmas nowadays, they would probably disown you.

So, we knew where technology levels were at, objects floating in the sky was definitely not normal. Nobody offered up any explanation. We just all stood in amazement as these things hovered around us high up in the sky. You didn't have camera on your phone, in fact, you didn't have a phone. A camera was a thing that was kept in a drawer in the house and required film. So, no pictures were taken. Eventually they hovered off, probably back to their planet to report there is no intelligent life on earth.

THE GREEN TRACKSUIT

Had not seen my tracksuit and Parka combo.

The grown-ups returned to the house, muttering that it had been interesting. We all stayed out, still amazed. What the bloody hell *was* that? None of us had any idea what it was. Were we about to get an Alien invasion? Maybe it had been the Ministry of Defence testing out some secret ship in the Highlands? I'm sure that could have happened. There are always reports of strange sightings going on in the night sky in the Highlands. There's such a big sky at night up North and very little light pollution, so you're more inclined to notice if there's a space ship following you home from the shops.

You had to get used to the dark up here, as you would spend a considerable amount of time wandering about in it. No room for fear of the dark in the country, you'd never go anywhere. Yes, you would spend a lot of your time tripping over shit, but you eventually got used to it, or you broke your leg.

I've never been scared of the dark. You can usually see more than you think once you get accustomed to it. And if there is a bad man lurking in the shadows ready to chop your head off, worrying about it isn't going to change the outcome, so you may as well enjoy yourself until you lose your head.

The journey home from the Maclean's in the car was full of much discussion about the strange objects in the sky. Mum on the other hand had got a new recipe, something to do with Venison and beetroot. We were just about home and Dad had just turned off the main road, when he said, 'what are those lights at Maggie's?' James and my ears pricked up. There were lights in the windows of Maggie's cottage and they were bright really bright and some were flashing and moving about. Dad slowed the car down and we all watched.

Dad switched off his car lights, and we all got out. The house was about a mile away from us but directly in front of us up on the hill. As soon as we all got out, the house went completely dark again. This house had no electricity. I don't even think it had water: there was a well out the back.

Mum said she hadn't seen Miss Mackenzie in a couple of months and she had mail that Maggie hadn't collected. Dad said he would go over in the morning and check everything was ok. Can we come said James? WE? I thought. What's with the *we* crazy brother? Don't bring me in to your certain death plan, that would involve journeying through the Dark Wood and then a visit to the house that everything tells me to stay away from. Fool, you can count me out! Call me mad, but I've had enough scary experiences for one night, without actively going and seeking out more. You Turnip!

The next morning, Dad and James were setting off for Maggie's. 'You coming, Pete?' said Dad. 'Ok.' I said.

What had I done? Bugger it!

Dad would be there: I'd be ok, this was the best time to go. I had to know what was going on over there. We all set off, through our wood then came to the gate to the Dark Wood. Dad opened it. We'd never been this far before. There was a narrow path through the woods. It gradually got darker the further in we got, the trees and bushes quite thick and overgrown. I was starting to feel uncomfortable. We'd never been to the Dark Wood before, and it smelt musty. We were half way, I was feeling ok, until James pointed out a large footprint in the mud.

Shit! I'd seen that before, and it was fresh. Just when I thought scary man had been erased from my consciousness, he was back in the blink of an eye, etched in mud. We kept on walking and were nearly there. We passed a huge rock that sat about twenty feet high, and as wide again, poking up out of the ground. It was a massive stone island covered in moss. I never knew that existed. This was like a completely different land. It was darker, denser and had a strangeness to it. I reminded myself that it was daylight and I was not alone.

Dad and James charged ahead with me tentatively bouncing along behind. As we grew closer, it started to get lighter as we neared the edge of the wood. Eventually, we emerged from the wood into the back garden that lay just behind the cottage. It had little flowers and what looked like herbs growing in the mossy over grown garden. There was a shed off to one side and a little path to the back door.

THE GREEN TRACKSUIT

James kept looking at me, I think he was excited at our first visit here. Me? Not so much.

Dad knocked on the little red door. The small porch was completely covered in ivy. You could barely see the door, let alone open it. The door that had once been red was now fading to pink. It had one lock on it and a black knob to open it. There was no answer.

'Let's go then,' I said and turned to leave.

'Wait,' said Dad. 'We'd better have a look around.'

The back of the cottage had two small windows with equally little curtains. The windows were dirty and difficult to see in. It was dark inside. I wasn't for looking but Dad and James were trying to peer in. I took a few steps back to examine the building. It had a corrugated iron roof which was covered in moss, a chimney pot on each end one which was broken. If this was the place of much evil then it didn't look that bad, with its nice little garden. But what was that horrible smell? It was awful and the further back I went the stronger it got, horribly strong. I was next to the shed. The door was slightly ajar. I pulled it open and the light shone in.

Hanging from the roof by a chain was a large animal carcass, I let out a scream.

'What is it?' shouted Dad as he made his way over. 'Oh, my God!' he said. 'What the hell is that?'

James had also arrived by now. 'That's a fox' said James.

There was a dead fox hanging by its back legs from a chain thrown over one of the beams, but more worrying than that was it had no head. Dad looked shocked. Who would do that? Yes, you shot things in the country but it was always humanely done. This was barbaric. There was a pile of blood directly beneath the poor animal, which looked like he had been there for a few weeks if not a month. We had now identified the victim as Mr Fox. No wonder we hadn't seen him in a while.

Dad stood and looked for a few minutes, then closed the door over again. He looked shocked and slightly embarrassed that someone would do that, and that we had seen it.

'Let's go,' he said sternly.

THE ALIENS ARE COMING

We all marched back through the woods in silence. It was obvious that Dad wasn't happy. He liked Mr Fox, when he wasn't eating our hens, and now he was dead and in such a brutal way. We returned through the woods at pace this time. Dad wasn't for talking. James and I remained silent as well, just the odd knowing glance to one another was enough. We knew what each other was thinking: Scary man had done this, and... where was the fox's head?

Dad went straight in the house. We stayed outside. A few hours later a police car arrived. Dad and the Policeman set off through the woods. We were told to stay at home. About half an hour later, Dad and the Policeman returned and went in the house. Shortly after, the Policeman left. James and I went in the house. Dad was having a cup of tea with Mum.

'What happened?' asked James.

Dad explained that when he had returned with the policeman to show him the fox, that it had *gone*. There was still blood on the floor but the fox had disappeared. The Policeman had believed Dad and said he would return in a few days and check again.

It was hard to believe that someone had removed it, in between us leaving Maggie's and Dad getting the Police. Even Dad thought we had been seen, and the culprit had removed the evidence before dad returned. Dad said we were not to go over there and if we saw anything we were to tell him. Now even the Police were involved. Bloody hell, this was getting serious.

James and I concluded that someone had been watching us when we were at Maggie's and they had removed the dead fox. Dad said that it was wildlife crime and that's why the police had come. He thought they wouldn't do anything about it. How could they? There was no evidence.

BABYSITTER

August would see the first ever Minster for Drought being appointed. Nicknamed 'Minister for Rain', Denis Howell was charged by the Prime Minister with the task of persuading the nation to use less water. 'Save water, bath with a friend' was his advice and this became the Summer's motto. I wasn't overly tempted, although it would certainly have moved a friendship along a bit.

'*Lovely of you to join me in the bath tonight, and may I say that's a lovely tattoo of a black widow spider you have there, Grandma.*'

'*It's not a tattoo. I sat on a grape at lunchtime.*'

'*Oh.*'

A bath was a special time, my alone time. Just me and my Action Man (Scuba Diver complete with dinghy. He had a torch, but I had lost it, I think it went down the plughole.) I wasn't for sharing my bath with anyone, not even a friend. Aren't we all missing the glaringly obvious here, you'd be *naked*. You may as well have been saying to your friends, '*Would you like to come to my house tonight and see me naked? Oh, and you can get naked too, yes? BFF's?*' (Bathing Friends Forever). That's a big step up from friends.

What if you fell out with them? In the bath, that's difficult. Imagine hurling insults at each other across the tub:

'*You know, one of your breasts is bigger than the other?*'

'*WHAT? Well, you've got a third nipple!*'

'*Get out of my bath! Call yourself a friend...*'

'*They look the same size to me.*'

BABYSITTER

'Well, they're NOT! And it's not a third nipple! It's a chocolate button I stuck on to make myself look more interesting. Look yum yum yum! Now put the dinghy down and get out of my bath!'

Dad and Mum would regularly share a bath together. I say share, but Dad would go in first, then he would get out and mum would get in. Sometimes there was a crossover period when they were both in the bath at the same time, which given the size of our bath was an achievement. I always assumed the splashing and giggling I could hear emanating from the bathroom was caused by their contortionist skills, but now I'm not so sure. Turns out the government were advising people to bath in five inches of water, so Dad and Mum realised if there were two of them in the bath then the water might come up to nearly their ankles. Genius! Still seemed to be a lot of giggling going on to me.

Five inches of water seems hardly worth taking your jumper off for. It's not like it was going to get wet. It would, however, certainly stop depressed farmers committing suicide by drowning themselves in the bath. That was going to be difficult now, in just five inches of water.

'Oh, for fuck sake! This is impossible! And now my pipe's gone out as well. I will just have to live another week then.'

If you had a big sponge and weren't careful you could find yourself sitting in an empty bath, looking at someone you didn't know very well.

'Oh, I meant to say, Mrs Urquart, I forgot to do my homework'

'See me after class!'

'Isn't that what we are doing? How much more would you like to see? Dental records?'

Alternatively, Mr Howell was actively encouraging people to shower with friends, two to be precise, I'm sure you could have more, but three in a shower was already going to be a squeeze. I suppose it all depended on the size of your shower, and your friends

'Hi Mary.'

'What can I do for you today, Peter?'

'Well, Mary, I was thinking about maybe having a shower tonight. I wondered if you and Betty from the freezer section fancied joining me, say eight o clock? Oh, and can you bring one of those multicoloured bars of melted down old soaps along too? I have a face cloth, and an Action man complete with dingy, what do you say?'

'Sorry Peter, but I had a bath last night with the coal man, and probably will again tonight. He's very dirty.'

'I bet he is, Mary. You're not going to be cold this winter then.'

'No, I suppose not.'

'What about Chilly Betty? She looks a bit grubby?'

'Now, I know she had a shower last night with the Campbell brothers, Peter.'

'Bloody hell! What about the chubby girl from the cake counter? She would definitely make the water level rise.'

'Sorry Peter, she's been having a bath with Dr Fergusson.'

'For God's sake! No wonder there's a water shortage. Everybody's at it. Oh well I will just leave it then. I'll just have the latest Look-In, Mary! I could start going to the Mace Shop you know. Bet someone would have a bath with me there.

'Well, they've been having a bath with—

'STOP MARY, just stop!' (STOMPS out of shop)

I imagine Duncan from the ironmongers was probably getting a waterfall installed in his house to take advantage of this situation

Anyway, the last thing on my mind was having a bath I was more concerned with trying to keep my head attached to my body, unlike Mr Fox. One thing was for sure Scary Man was back. There was no doubt about that. Just when I had forgotten about him as well. Bugger! The Wheelie Pack were summonsed, and we convened in the new hut- the one we *hadn't* built naked- which was now a bit too close to the dark wood. When will we learn" We told them of the morning's events at Maggie's cottage, at which point Euan remembered another family outing he had forgotten about and left, rather quickly again. We know you don't have a family outing, Euan. I thought, we are not completely stupid...well... James isn't.

'Where you going Euan? A roller disco, that would be great?' I love a roller disco, oh yeah, he's lying. Damn it. I was looking forward to that.

Peter Easton was all for going over there and punching Scary Man right now. The rest of us didn't think that was the best approach, although I thought it was a good idea. I wanted this over and sorted. I was fed up being scared; I had only just got used to not shitting myself on a daily basis, and I wasn't going back to that. We decided the adults weren't going to sort this, so we would have to. Hoping it would go away wasn't an option anymore.

So far, he had taken great delight in scaring me half to death on the road that night, and now he had chopped the head off Mr fox, and let's not forget all the flashing lights that we had seen from the road. I'm not even going to think about where Miss Mackenzie was? Nobody seemed concerned at all that we hadn't seen her, all we knew was she wasn't at the cottage. Mum suggested she might have gone to stay with her sister, although she wasn't a hundred percent sure that her sister was still alive. If not, she wasn't going to be great company. (More tea Sister? Silence, Please yourself!) Wherever she was the best thing she could do was stay there away from this horrible place. Unless of course she is locked in a wardrobe with a fox's head, I thought. I suspect she had been scared away. I hoped she had, unless she really was a witch, and Scary was her wizard son who had come home to murder the locals starting with ME.

Hello Mother, that's me back from wizard university, Welcome home Son, now would you like a spot of killing with your old mother before tea, oh yes please mother, but who, what about that annoying boy that lives next door the one that's always flashing his bum and never eats my poisoned pan drops, oh yes please mother. Good lad, I'm very proud of you son. Whose is all that washing? That's mine mother, oh for fuck sake, and I just put a blood-stained wash on.

We were going to find him and confront him and if necessary take him down. That's assuming he didn't find me first. There were four of us, and he looked a bit skinny. Surveillance of the dark wood was on and under way. We had the perfect look out from our new hut. First, we put a large lock on the inside of the hut so we could lock ourselves in, then we set about gathering our supply of weapons. The hut was well stocked just in case. We also tied fishing gut to some old tin cans and set a perimeter round the hut. If anyone came near they would trip on the fishing line and trigger our alarm. This was on!!!

Everyone tripped over that fishing line, it was too good. You would always forget about it; the tin cans were forever rattling. It sounded like Mardi Gras in the woods that summer.

Oh, for Fuck sake! Who put that there? Oh yeah... we did.

Three days passed, then a week and still nothing. This was getting boring. We were manning the hut between the four of us most of the day, sometimes till late at night. There were always two there, no one wanted to do it alone. Euan hadn't been seen, he was definitely out. Maybe he had a bad fall at the Roller Disco?

Peter Easton turned up one morning for the usual hut shift, with some interesting news. The previous night his parents had been out and he had a babysitter. She and Peter had stayed up late talking and telling ghost stories. *WAIT A MINUTE! The Wheelie king has a babysitter*! I was slightly shocked: His Majesty could not be left alone. I'm not going to say I wasn't disappointed. This was sad news indeed, anyway.

A babysitter was generally someone who came around, ate all your biscuits, ignored you, then sent you to bed. But Emma hadn't been like that at all. Peter had told her of my encounter with Mr Scary. She was very interested and said if he had been a ghost then the best way to contact him was with a Ouija board. What the fud was a Ouija board? Peter explained it was a board with letters on it and yes and no on it too. You asked it questions, and the glass in the middle which everybody had one finger on would move and spell out answers. So...not creepy in the slightest then.

We were out of ideas, anything was worth a try and it seemed like a good idea. *No, it bloody didn't.* But where the fud would we get one? I doubt the local Spar shop in the village sold them. I was boycotting the Spar anyway, due to the bathing incident, or lack of it. I'd have to get my Look-In magazine elsewhere from now on. I was now hanging out at the Ironmongers now. (This is a man's world)

They had everything in the Ironmongers and the shop went on for ever. You could get lost in there. You'd occasionally meet someone through the back, ranting and raving about how they had come in for a candle on Tuesday and got lost. *'Have I missed Christmas?'*

It was run by Duncan the local Casanova of the Highlands, and he made sure you knew it too.

'Hello Peter. Have you seen my new tight extra tight jeans?'

'Oh, wow! Yes, they are tight Duncan! Boiled eggs for breakfast?

'How did you know?'

'I think I can see one.'

'Oh, I also had a sausage Peter.'

'I'm aware of that Duncan. I was wondering if you had a Ouija board currently in stock? What might that retail at, oh tight-trousered Duncan?'

'Ouija, you say Peter? Is it something to do with girls?'

No that wasn't going to work, this was the Occult, a tool for witchcraft and the dark arts. The village could be weird and I grant you some of them looked half dead, but this might have been a step too far, even for them.

James could make a Ouija board. We could certainly make one. It can't be that hard, we thought; a bit of wood and a pen and we would be fine. Now, I would not advise anyone to make a Ouija board. It's used for trying to contact the spirits of the dead, it's not like Mouse Trap at all. The process of making it is scary enough without ever using it, but we were desperate. James cut a piece of wood in to a large square shape. He was even sanded the edges. We were trying to contact the dead; a splinter was the last of our worries. Then we drew the letters on and put a yes and no on either side of the centre, and it also had to have hello and goodbye on it, just to be polite I suppose. It was complete, now all we had to do was use it… mmm, that was a thought. Peter said spirits don't come out during the day only at night. 'They do in the village.' I thought. So, we had to do it at night, great. Could this get any better?!

Peter was due to have a further babysitting evening, and Emma

THE GREEN TRACKSUIT

the sitter held the knowledge of all things Occult. He would get more information on how exactly we used it. Twice he'd had a babysitter, he was going down in my estimations by the minute.

A few days later he returned with the desired information. The Séance (which, I discovered, is what you call the process of try to contact the dead) would take place that evening, which also happened to be a full moon. Brilliant, I'll change my pants now then.

Oh, whoop de doo! I can't wait, I thought. Still, it seemed better than running scared all my days, although that was looking like a better option. It would take place in the hut when it was dark, by candle light. I think you needed candles as part of the process. Why don't we just get a fox's head in to the bargain? We could make fox head soup while we are at it! "

"More Fox head soup Hector, or what about some more bread, fox bread obviously, but I think its gluten free, it's not hair free though"

Nine o clock arrived, the arranged time. Hector and Peter Easton were both going to stay the night at ours, so they didn't have to travel home alone. Who knew how long this would take. I've never tried to contact the dead before… might take a while.

We all assembled in the hut, and lit four candles, one for each of us, James produced his Ouija board, which was a master piece as usual, although it looked quite scary. He had even varnished it.

I suppose so it lasted and we could get continued use out of it for years to come, I told you he was weird, who in their right mind varnishes a Ouija board, two coats apparently!!, my brother.

I don't know if you've ever had the pleasure of sitting in a hut with a Ouija board in candlelight before. It is bed-wettingly scary. Peter Easton was our spokesman. He would ask the questions, since he knew the most about it. We all had to put one finger on the small glass, which we had stolen- I mean borrowed- from the house. This sat in the centre of the board. Hopefully it would move. I say hopefully, but I was hoping it didn't.

'Silence'… said Peter Easton. He was taking it very seriously. Peter piped up 'Is there anybody there?' in his best ghostly voice.

We all pissed ourselves laughing. Of course, there is! James, me and Hector are here, you dick! *Sorry Peter, didn't mean to call you a dick...I said,* He asked again: nothing. All our laughter had gone now and we were all starting to take it seriously.

'We wish to contact a spirit at Maggie's,' Peter said.

Good questioning. The glass slid and stopped on HELLO. We all removed our fingers immediately. That was a bit quick. I had definitely felt something, a bit like electricity, as the glass moved. I did wonder if it was another one of James's electrocution jobs again. The problem with this is anyone of the four of us could help the glass move. You could only be sure that it wasn't you, so there was a lot of trust involved. Everyone swore they hadn't helped it move. Reluctantly we all put our fingers back on.

'Why are you here?' asked Peter.

The glass slid first to C then to U and R then S and E... CURSE.

I had hoped it was a spelling mistake and should have spelt Purse; maybe the spirit had lost it a few years earlier and had come back to look for it. Nobody moved and we were completely silent, just looking at one another, hoping this could be over. Peter was just about to ask his next probing question, when the glass fell over by itself and rolled off the board and smashed.

That was enough. Hatch open and out of the hut, we were all running back to the house full speed. Once inside we locked the door.

OK, what had we learned? There's a curse and he wants us to come to Maggie's and look for it. That was the consensus. Let me think... mmm... you can bugger right off. I never wanted to see that Ouija board again ever, even if it has been varnished. Even my track suit couldn't take any more of this, enough! I decided someone had been moving the glass, probably James- this was his style- or maybe Peter Easton since he had come up with idea to start with. Definitely not Hector, he looked traumatised by the whole thing. Nobody was without suspicion, somebody had done it.

'There's no such thing as ghosts, no such thing, they don't exist, ok? Oh, crap and bollocks what if they do? No such thing, just someone playing a prank, don't rise to Peter. I'm going to have to

think about this for a couple of days. If you need me I will be under the bed thinking, so if you don't mind I'd rather be alone...'

A few days passed and I eventually emerged from my bedroom, I hadn't been sleeping well, I couldn't go on like this. I had made my mind up. We were going to Maggie's again and I would go alone if I had to. Turns out I wasn't the only one having nightmares. None of us had been sleeping well. Euan had returned. We told him about our Séance. He was about to leave, when I said Euan we need you to stay, five is a much better number. He agreed and said he would stay, but openly admitted he was scared.

'We are all scared,' said Peter Easton, 'but together we are stronger.' Peter was scared? First the babysitter, now this. This was altogether rather disappointing.

Mum was going to be raging when she found out we had broken her glass! We would have to lie and say it wasn't us, *'What glass, Mum? I think I saw Lynn with it and a bottle of Baileys I could have be mistaken though, might have been Tia Maria.'* Anyway, it wasn't a lie we hadn't broken it. The Scary Man had... sort of.

SHARN

We would return to Maggie's today; there were five of us, we were strong in numbers and it was daytime. Although Dad had told us not to go over to Maggie's, we were going. It had to be done or none of us were ever going to sleep again, and I liked sleeping. It was one of the things I was particularly good at.

Another was that I was capable of eating four Wagon Wheels back to back, known as 'the double axel'. Back then, Wagon Wheels were a lot bigger. Mr. Burton claims that Wagon Wheels haven't got smaller: it is merely our hands have got bigger from when we were children. That may be the case Mr. Burton, but that wasn't my unit of measurement. It was a well-known fact that a Wagon Wheels in the Seventies was the same size as a baby's head. It had been scientifically proven using a Wagon Wheel and a baby's head. Are we to believe that babies heads have also decreased in size as well as your biscuits? Burton, I still like your biscuits though, your advertising slogan was "you've got to grin to get it in" it's less of a grin these days, more of a smirk.

We would not go through the Dark Wood though, that might be too much. There was another way, through the fields, and it was a lot more open. That way, we would see if anyone was approaching. At the corner of our road there was a path that lead up to the cottage, a small muddy path took you to the field in front of Maggie's. Then we would climb up to the cottage, it was a lot less scary that way. We all set off, the pace was slow and Euan was at the back. I would be surprised if he didn't head home to another Roller Disco. *oh can I come? I will get my skates I just need to unscrew them from this piece of wood then we can be off, oh yeah,*

THE GREEN TRACKSUIT

I've done it again.

Eventually we reached the gate to the field in front of Maggie's. We all stopped and looked up the hill. It was sunny, but the cottage at the edge of the wood still looked dark and foreboding. Its two little windows looked dark as always. It had a barbed wire fence round the front, but within it all looked still. So, we all climbed over the gate and started up the hill, the field was full of cows, about twenty. We knew cows, this was not a problem, slow lethargic animals, perfectly harmless.

As we neared the top we could see the house in much more detail. From the front, you could see where the front door had been bricked up, but it hadn't been done very well. It was a bit of a rough job: James would not have approved of such poor craftsmanship. We all surveyed this scary looking house. No wonder people didn't like to come here. It looked gruesome: let's face it, a barbed wire fence round your house isn't very inviting. There were two small windows upstairs. I never realised the cottage had an upstairs. All the windows were grubby and you could barely see anything through them. We climbed the fence and tried to look in carefully to check if the coast was clear. I could see a table and a chair and there was an old range, but it was so dark. There didn't seem to be anyone here.

James and Peter Easton had headed round to the back door, the one we had gone to with Dad. This was the only door in or out of this ghastly cottage. We all followed round slowly. We had agreed that if anything happened we would go back the same way we had come, and not go through the dark wood. Above all, we must not split up under any circumstances: that was a priority.

The door looked as we had left it with Dad, closed and scary. We all headed to the shed to see if Dad had been right and the fox had gone. Euan and I were to stay back and keep lookout. I was to watch the door of the cottage and Euan was to watch the field at the front. We didn't want any surprises. We took up our positions. James, Peter Easton and Hector approached the shed. I was watching the door, which I had just noticed had a large cobweb on it. This door hadn't been opened in a while that was for sure, and a relief. Where ever Miss Mackenzie was, she hadn't been here. I was keeping one eye on the door and one on the shed. I noticed something moving in the garden.

It was just a pheasant, but it was golden. We had heard there was a golden pheasant in these woods, but we had never seen it. It was literally sparkling as it wandered in and out of the dappled sunlight. It was startled by something and flew off. I was quite chuffed at seeing this. These are rare birds and I've never seen one since.

I looked back to the boys at the shed, they had gone. WHAT! I looked back to the door, it was still closed, but wait, the cobweb had gone. I ran around the front to where Euan was, he had gone too. Fudding hell! They were all running down the field. I jumped the fence and took off at pace. My advice, if you see everyone else running, is run. There's generally a good reason so RUN! The cows were going nuts and seemed to be chasing me down the field. Cows didn't do this! What happened to being slow and lethargic? These were bloody racing cows and they were gaining on me.

The boys were now at the gate and were clear. They were watching my progress and I was only half way down the field, with a herd of angry racing cows chasing me. I was at full speed and they were gaining on me. I went in to turbo mode, a rarely used running mode that was fast but not without risk. It could only be sustained for short periods of time and could prove to be very volatile, a bit like nitrous oxide for cars, that can blow your engine up. My feet were going so fast I lost control of them and started to slide. I fell on my back but was still sliding down the field at speed. I felt a splatter and something hit my face. I could barely see, but got up and ran to the gate and jumped it just before the cows arrived.

All I could hear was laughter. I wiped the mud from my face and looked at my hand that wasn't mud! This was shit and it stank. I was covered from head to toe in cow shite (sharn to country folk). My green tracksuit was completely covered. The boys were lying on the ground completely wetting themselves. I've never seen four boys laugh so much in my life. We had gone from fear to hysterical laughter. Well, *I* wasn't laughing.

Clearly when I had fallen I had slid through a cow's shit. It had been large and freshly made, and had the consistency of double cream. It really stank and I was completely covered. This hadn't just been a large cow shit: this had been the largest shit a cow had ever done in the history of cow shits. Eventually the boys managed to gain the ability to walk again, although every few steps they would burst out in to laughter and start rolling about again.

'Why did you all run?' I asked. They had been startled when the pheasant flew off and they legged it. Euan had just followed the others. You could have told me! They had thought I was behind them. Well, I was but in a bath of shit. I can still smell it now, God it stank.

The journey back to the house took a lot longer than normal, due to the fact we had to stop every two minutes so that everyone could roll about laughing again. I'm sure it was hilarious had you not been the one who was covered in shit. I gave up waiting on them and went home alone. To be greeted by more laughter, from Dad and Mum who also thought this was the funniest day of their life.

I had to undress outside, just to add insult to my misery. Dad hosed me down, with cold water, while pissing himself laughing. Really could this day get any worse? Then, I had to walk on newspaper mum had put down on the floor through to the shower. At one point, she was on her hands and knees crying with laughter, and had to be helped up by Dad who was also in fits of laughter.

Family who needs them! As soon as I had raised enough money picking raspberries, I was out of there! I had already saved seventy-eight pounds. I was dripping in money; well, actually, I was dripping in shit. I spent a considerable amount of time in the shower (alone). After several showers I could still smell the sharn, and I could still hear the laughter from the kitchen. Not my finest hour, but everyone else was having the funniest day of their life. I know we are supposed to laugh at our failings but this was not one of these times, and although I wanted to laugh I couldn't.

This event would be relived many times, for many years. 'Remember the time Peter fell in shite?' Yes, I do, thank you. I was unlikely to forget it; I could still smell it.

I heard Mum had even started recounting the story to her patients when she was doing her rounds. This was the best medicine they'd had in ages, and the ones who weren't already wetting themselves were now wetting themselves laughing, at my expense. It appeared that half of Inverness-Shire knew the story. I was a legend in some quarters, mainly with the elderly, thanks to mum.

For a while there if you opened the window late at night, you could hear the distant sound of people pissing themselves laughing at Sharn Boy. It appeared that despite there being millions of cows shites in the country, I was the only person that this had ever happened to. Hurray, go me.

Mum said she had even told Mary at the Spar. Mary said she hadn't seen me in a while. Truth be told I was starting to miss her; the way she would angrily punch the numbers in to the till, how she would shout 'PRICE, LINDA!' at the top of her voice... aww Mary. I remembered the time I didn't have enough money to buy the Arctic Roll I had selected for my lunch. I was three pence short. Mary just smiled at me with a slight hint of moustache and said, 'On you go, Peter.' That was Mary.

'I'll get it next time,' and she did.

'You owe me three pence, Elliot!'

Aww... Mary.

Mum said she hadn't seen her at the Scottish Country Dance Class that week. Maybe Mary was depressed? Mary loved the Scottish Country Dance Class. All the ladies in the village did, and went every Thursday to the Kilmorack Hall without fail. None of the men went. Well... a few who lacked the strength to tell their partners they would rather have a vasectomy than go, were dragged along.

There would be about fifty middle-aged (if you were lucky) tartan clad rampant women, and maybe three petrified men. A man to dance with was a treat, as most weeks the ladies would all have to dance with each other. which made it more like a LGBT get together than a dance.

Many of the ladies were single as well, so this was their only chance to get to touch a man, hold a man in their arms, get up close and personal to the big hairy beast again. They certainly made the most of it. The men were in high demand, and the stale smell of whisky and roll ups filled the air, and that was just the women.

It was terrible what they did to those poor spineless men, week after week they passed them around like a bag of Soor Plooms. Which is slightly ironic, as if they had the vasectomy they would have had Soor Plooms anyway. Strip the Willow? They did a lot more than just bloody strip the willow.

I did miss Mary, and the Ironmongers wasn't as much fun as I had hoped it would be. I was continually getting lost, and Duncan would just appear from nowhere.

'Hello, Peter!'

'Jesus, Duncan! Where did you come from?'

'Screws .... and nails, through the back, second right, first left, past the gas bottles four left first right, you can't miss it. Have you seen my new super tight T-shirt Peter?'

'Yes, that is tight Duncan.'

'And my extra tight tight jeans?'

'Yes Duncan. Wow, they look even tighter today.'

'I can't get them off. I actually can't, it's hilarious! I'm thirty-six. How old do you think I am Peter? Thirty-four? I know, its bloody brilliant! Oh, must go, I think I can see a girl browsing the camping equipment ..

"now are you looking for a two man or a four man the two man's very cosy, do come in....'

And off he would mince in his slip-on clogs and funny walk like he constantly needed to go to the toilet. He was weird, but oddly the women seemed to like him. Rumour has it he had a shag pile carpet and a water bed, no wonder they liked him and probably a very large shower, just sayin.

Obviously, we hadn't told Dad and Mum where Sharngate had happened. We had many fields and there was always plenty shite in the country. We just didn't always wear it. My poor tracksuit. It had seen a lot and saved me from so much. Mum said it would have to go in the bin. It couldn't be the end of it. I needed it, without it I was vulnerable. We would have to go back to Maggie's. I needed it more than ever now. Yes, it barely fitted anymore and did look a bit the worse for wear, I knew all this but I was not done with it yet, we still had work to do. Mum even said she would buy me a new one. New was a rare thing in the country.

No, I said, and begged her to wash it. She wasn't keen but eventually agreed. I think she washed it several times and then put the washing machine on with nothing in it, to clean the machine. Just to be sure, the things Mums have to do.

Who knew a tracksuit could mean so much? When you're nine the strangest things are important to you, and this was important.

Sharngate, (literally, since I fell in Sharn then jumped a gate,) had one plus: it had made us all less scared of going to Maggie's cottage. It had been the scene of much laughter, well for everybody else it had. We had spooked ourselves that day and we had all panicked. We were not going to find out much behaving like that, but now everybody was less scared and that could only be a good thing. I was still convinced the spiders web had disappeared, but never said anything. I couldn't see how that was possible, and no one was going to listen to SHARN boy, which everyone took great delight in calling me. I didn't care: I was a legend in some old folks' homes. *I was actually keeping people alive, old people were only staying alive to see what stupid thing I would get up to next.*

Euan said he had seen a flag pole and flag in the woods, behind Maggie's, when he had been on look out. This was hard to believe, but he was adamant. We decided to investigate. We went back to the field in front of Maggie's, where I had become Sharn boy. And true enough there was an orange flag complete with pole behind the house, further up in the dark wood. How had we not seen this? There wasn't a house up there. We knew that it was just woods, and if somebody had built a house we would have known. James and I concluded that it must have been on top of the rock island that we had seen when going through the dark wood with Dad. Maybe it was just a flag pole and nothing else, or maybe Scary Man was staying there.

The only two ways to get to it were, up through the field past

THE GREEN TRACKSUIT

Maggie's (sharn field) and in to the dark wood, or from ours through our wood then the gate, and in to the dark wood. We decided to go the way we had gone with Dad. I'd had enough of cows, and this might give us the element of surprise.

We all set off without incident. No one was moaning or bottling out of it. We were getting used to wandering about the woods being scared. We all marched through the wood laughing and joking, then we came to the stone island. It was massive, even bigger than I remembered. There were big massive trees growing on top. It was so big, there seemed to be no way up it. The rock was almost vertical and covered in moss, so slippy.

Eventually, we found a path behind some bushes, not easy to find, and it was still a steep climb. We all made it to the top. This rock was massive. The top which was flat must have been the size of a tennis court, huge. And there in the centre beneath a huge tree was a small house, about the size of a caravan, made from old bits of wood and sheets of corrugated iron. Hard to believe that if this hadn't had a flag pole we would never have found it. From up here you could see the entire wood.

There were no windows but one small door, with a wire hook to keep it shut. We opened it and looked in. The walls, ceiling and floor were bright orange. On closer inspection, they had been lined with old fertiliser bags. We all went inside. This was a work of art. Each plastic fertiliser bag had been folded and carefully nailed in position and so on. It was like tiles on a roof and completely water tight, and very warm. The five of us sat in the hut, examining the inside. It was very bright, the orange was slightly over powering, I think I'm blind, but still it was cool.

Who had built this? and why? This went way beyond hut building, it must have taken ages. The flag pole that had led us here also had an orange fertiliser bag nailed on it at height. Why go to all the trouble of building this where it could never be found, then put up a big bloody orange flag? There was nothing inside it and nothing outside it that made you think anyone had been here in a while; no foot prints, no rubbish…nothing. This made no sense.

The hut must have only been three or four hundred yards from our house and slightly closer to Maggie's maybe two hundred yards away. We left, but set up a few traps. We would return in a couple of days and check if anyone had been here. There was much deliberation as to who and why this had been built, but James insisted no one person could have built the hut. The size of the some of the pieces of wood required at least two people to get them up to the top of that rock. And James knew- he was the inventor of all things, and had electrocuted me several times in doing so. Mainly the hovercraft that had previously been a hoover. That was the source of much electrocution for me, being mains powered and all, but he had never killed me yet, and I trusted his judgement, if not his wiring.

Maybe it had been a rival gang, of which there were few, if any. This wasn't exactly Harlem. Again, James insisted this was not the work of kids. Ok, so some adults built a secret hut on top of a rock then put up a big bloody flag pole and then buggered off, never to return to it. Euan suggested it might have been a wood choppers house. This wasn't Little Red Riding Hood where there were wood choppers living in the woods. We *wood* have known about that, boom boom... Sorry, Euan good idea... well not really, but least he was still here. Had it been a hide for shooting Deer? That was a better idea, but we would have heard the gun shoots and nobody shot here. Remember, it was very close to Maggie's as well.

The only solution we could come up with was that it had been a hut, that someone had built and they had abandoned it. We did that all the time, although this had been a particularly good hut. I'm not sure we would have left a hut this good. Mind you, I'm not sure we could have built a hut this good, no offence James. In time, we would find out if anyone was staying there, until then we would keep watch on it from a distance. I still can't believe we were building all these huts over the Summer when three hundred yards from our house was the most fantastic hut we had ever seen. It was virtually impossible to find. If you took down that flag nobody would ever find it. I still couldn't understand the flag, it made no sense.

The new find was under surveillance, and every couple of days

THE GREEN TRACKSUIT

we would check our traps to see if anyone had been there. We had rested a small twig at the bottom of the door of the hut. If the door opened, the twig would move. Simple. We had done a similar thing resting a small stick at the bush that hid the path. Any movement would be detected. Every couple of days the traps were checked. This did mean a regular trip to the dark wood but we were getting used to it, and we were more excited about our new find. We wanted to claim this as ours and the longer it was undisturbed the more likely that became. The first thing I would do is take down that bloody flag. We could have amazing fun with the new secret location. Nobody would ever find us up there, and even if they could, getting up to it was next to impossible. It was perfect.

G & G

Unfortunately, our surveillance of the hut would have to be put on hold, as we had to endure our annual pilgrimage to Rockhaven to see The Grandparents. Both my mum and dad's parents still stayed there. Mum's parents were to be called Granda and Grannie. This was the Army Granda, who insisted you have your top off at the first sight of sun, and was hell-bent on us getting skin cancer before we were twenty, maybe earlier. And Dad's parents insisted on being called Papa and Grans (stepmother, wicked variety).

What a bloody nonsense, can't you all just be called the same? I'm nine for God sake and don't have time for this shit. I've a Scary Man in my life. I would regularly forget and call someone Prams or Panda or worse.

Thank you for the birthday present Fanny... I mean Grannie, and you too Bandy... sorry, Granda.

It would become easier in time when there were fewer of them, and I was left with fewer names to choose from. but for now, I had four grandparents all with different names! Can't I just call you all OLD?

I think Dads parents thought Papa and Grans was posher: it was all about that with Grans, the wicked witch. She was never a Grans, certainly not to me - she was definitely a Grandmother and a wicked one at that. Grans are friendly little old ladies who smelt of lavender and spat on tissues and then proceeded to wipe it all over your face, I think it was to build up your immune system. Or maybe they just liked spitting ? They knitted you hats. *She* wasn't going to knit you a hat. I would remain Hatless. They were quite posh, but there was no need to make us call you stupid names.

THE GREEN TRACKSUIT

I remember once being left there myself for a few days- hell on earth, I took a pancake at the dinner table one night and put jam on it. (Mum had fuelled my jam addiction). You'd have thought I had set light to the curtains.

'You don't have jam till after you've had your dinner Peter!'

Really? Well, I was just trying to eat something before the main course arrived because after I've eaten that I will probably feel sick and won't be able to eat anything else. Obviously, I didn't say that, but it was ridiculous. She wasn't a nice woman, hadn't been to Dad and wasn't to us, and Papa would just sit there and say nothing, Old people really are bonkers.

Anyway, it was a yearly thing that none of us really wanted to do. It had been fine when we were small and did what we were told, but now we were getting bored of being stripped half naked and ordered about. Once Mum's Dad 'Army Granda' was watching the bird table out our kitchen window at the Birches over breakfast and said, and I quote,

'That's a lovely pair of Tits you've got there, Anne.'

James and I started pissing ourselves laughing. He stormed out, got Granny and left. We didn't see them for three years. What were we supposed to think? Really, we were kids and that was very funny. I still laugh when I hear the word TIT. Not because it is a slang word for breast, but because I remember Granda saying it to mum. Hilarious. Three years? Really.

The journey to Rockhaven was long and the yellow Volvo 144 saloon was cramped for five, and there was always one who was travel sick. Oh yeah… that was me.

'Must have been the four Wagon Wheels I had in Fochabers.'

And just in case that wasn't bad enough, behind us was Dad and Mums favourite caravan, well it had to be, we only had one. At the mere mention of the word *caravan*, we would all burst in to singing The Caravan Song by Barbara Dickson.

Caravans, oh my soul is on the run Overland, I am flying...

At fifty miles an hour!! On the A96 with about thirty cars behind us all getting increasingly pissed off. We didn't care we were too busy singing, which I don't think helped as they were overtaking us giving us evils, when we are all in full song

Caravans moving out into the sun. Oh, I don't know where I'm going... but I'm going

We knew where we were going we just weren't going there very fast. I'm ashamed to admit it now, but yes, we were CARAVANERS! In the Seventies, this was the pastime of Kings. Caravaners were seen as Gods, hailed as pioneers, with their awnings and chemical toilets like mobile houses. People would stop and clap as you drove through the villages and towns. You were Royalty in one of these, Trailer Royalty not Trash.

A house you could take with you, where ever you wanted to go was the eighth wonder of the modern world. Well, sort of... No foreign trips for us, this was it. We didn't do it often, thank God, five in a caravan was a stretch to say the least. It was great when you were four years old but when you were teenagers, not so much.

We would make many trips to Rockhaven. It was a nice town and beside the sea which was something new for us. We would do the usual visits to each grandparent's house, but we never saw them together. There must have been a reason for that, maybe they didn't get on, who knows? Old people are funny things, always a bit grumpy and bossy especially when there is jam involved.

We would always stay in the caravan park on our trips" valley of the Kings". Mums' parents, Grannie and Granda, didn't have the room for us to stay, and Dads, Grans and Papa, had the room but didn't want us there. That kind of summed them up; they were posh, and didn't really have time for kids, not even their own. We would have to go there for dinner and sit nicely on the Pouffe and answer all the question politely.

'How's School?'
'Fine thanks, Fanny.'
The usual stuff.

The food would always be awful, Oxtail soup was one particularly bad memory, but there were many to choose from, and you had to eat it, I still can't eat soup, that ruined soup forever for me. Thanks Grans.

Mums parents were better, a bit more fun, providing the sun

wasn't out or Granda would insist you were half naked. (When I look back now it was rather odd behaviour, but he did collect golf balls and didn't play golf, that's what you do when you're old). Granny was very quiet. She just obeyed orders.

'Tea?'
'Yes, James.'
'Knitted Hat?'
'No, Peter.'

We would go to Skatie Shore, a beach not far from their house. A beach was a novelty for us country types.

'What's that grainy stuff?'
'That's sand, Peter.'
'Look a pterodactyl!'
'No, that's a seagull.'
'Oh...'

Still, it was good fun. Everything was always a bit of a military excise with Granda. I remember once having to abseil down the cliffs to get to the beach. There was a path.

'It's just over there Granda, look! People are using it to get to the beach.'
'NO! JUMP!'

On another occasion, we were heading back at high tide and got stranded on some rocks. We could have all drowned, but we didn't. That was the Seventies! Yes, you could have died, but you didn't. It was always good fun and we learnt a lot from them. I've never had to use the abseiling yet, but you never know. JUMP

I think the trips were always a bit stressful for Dad and Mum, visiting parents and all that. Papa was chairman of the RNLI in Rockhaven, so we would get trips out on the lifeboat. Now, *that* was exciting! Bouncing about the sea with a full crew, all dressed in wet weather gear. Fly fishing was another great love of Papa's. Sometimes we would be woken up in the middle of the night to go fly fishing. I never caught anything, but I once had a fish on the line, but it got away. It was always fun, although would have been more fun if we had caught something. Obviously, James did! Tit.

Papa was a nice man when you got him away from Grans, but

he was spineless, and bossed by Granny who was one broom stick away from being a witch. I always thought if she and Army Granda had got together, they would have been a formidable force, and probably could have invaded and taken over most of Europe. Who knows our national food could have been oxtail soup? It would certainly have made the enemy talk, or throw up. We could have become a nation of bird watchers who collected golf balls. I wasn't going to suggest the wife swap. In the interests of world peace, best to keep them apart. They'd probably had enough of that in the sixties anyway.

So, visits to Rockhaven were always fun, if somewhat bizarre, with our weird grandparents. After the bird table incident when Granda stormed off because we laughed at his Tit comment we didn't see him for over three years, during which time they never spoke to us. For three years, he was raging. That just shows how out of touch he was with reality, although he did know his birds.

He also once went mental again because someone took a banana from the fruit bowl without asking. It turned in to a big thing. It was like the Cuban missile crisis... well, it was to him. We were all individually questioned as to whether we had seen a banana and if so, had we eaten it?

I was in the clear: I didn't like bananas. This didn't stop me being interrogated, in case I had been pretending all these years I didn't like bananas just so I could pull off the perfect crime. I think I said it wasn't me, must have been one of the other bunch... which didn't help.

It was completely ridiculous. You put the fruit bowl on the table. There was no sign saying eat at your own risk. People get locked up for less nowadays. I should have phoned ChildLine but they hadn't been invented yet.

Anyway, I'm pretty sure it was James. He had a penchant for bananas, and he did always say he had a pet gorilla in the woods that he used to take it a piece of bread for from the house. I thought maybe the banana was for him. He never confessed to it, probably just as well. After Banana Gate, we only went to visit Granda and Grannie with Dad and Mum. It wasn't deemed safe for us to go alone. Maybe Grannie had eaten it? She was never questioned. Just a thought, maybe *she* had pulled off the perfect crime? For forty years, she had been lying in wait, pretended to be a nice old lady, waiting for her moment to pull of the heist of the century. To this day, Banana Gate remains unsolved. The skin was never found, probably buried in a shallow grave in the woods, and nobody ever came forward. The case remains open.

This trip had passed without incident. We had done the usual stuff, been thrown off cliffs with only a rope and marched about half naked trying to get skin cancer, oh and eaten disgusting food. We would always have to go to Crathes Castle before we went home so Dad and Mum could fill the caravan up with plants and probably fruit bushes for the garden. Our caravan on the return journey always looked more like a mobile greenhouse than a caravan, but still people clapped when we drove through... and still we sang.

Our trips away were always fun: Dad made it that way. He saw the best in everything, not so much in Granda, or Grans the witch, but he always did his best to make it fun for us.

Later in life I would end up moving to Rockhaven and still stay there today. If only I could remember where I buried that banana.

Rockhaven is a nice place: beautiful in summer, hell- hole in the winter. Next to the sea it gets very cold, and the town is still full of mad people and lots of pensioners who you will regularly see in the Co-op shouting at a pork pie. Must be something in the sea air that makes them go nuts. Anyway, soon I will be able to do that. I'm quite looking forward to being old and grumpy and mad about everything. The shouting at food thing might be fun.

'Bugger off sausages! I hate you!'
'Screw you, broccoli! You cruciferous bastard!'
And fuck you fromage frais, in your tiny pots
Something to look forward to

We were on our way home, caravan fully loaded with plants, kids suitably exhausted from near death experiences… A good time had been had by all. We had survived another trip to see The Grandparents. It was only a matter of time before Granda manufactured a gun out of old golf balls, or Grans started poisoning the jam, but for now all was well. *Hurray, we didn't die at Grannie and Granda's* was the song we used to sing in our yellow Volvo 144 saloon heading Northwards. The chorus was *who's got the banana*?

As soon as we had arrived home and emptied the forty thousand plants out of the caravan, James and I headed to the hut. We carefully inspected our clever traps. Nobody had been there. Brilliant, that was the news we wanted. The Wheelie Pack were summonsed and we all agreed the hut was now ours. We would take it over on the grounds it was empty. If nobody had been there in two weeks, it was rightfully ours, according to country law Act 6271 the 1973 hut abandonment ACT. ref 212. Not to be confused with the 1973 wigwam act. Ref 213.

This was brilliant. We now had the best hut for miles if not in the whole of Inverness-shire. Best of all, nobody would ever find it, apart from the person or persons who had built it and they were long gone, we hoped. From here we could watch the woods and more importantly Maggie's, from a safe location. We just hoped Scary Man didn't know about the hut. First thing we did was get that bloody flag down, which was very high, but we managed. Now it was impossible to find... where's the Bloody hut?

THE CURSE

My tracksuit was back and clean, lying folded on the bed. It had a strange smell now, always the distant smell of shite, and with the continual washes it was smaller than ever. The trousers were almost three quarter length, the sort that England football fans wear on their holidays. They look ridiculous. I think Beckham had worn a pair of these stupid trousers, and as usual the rest of the country followed, well England did. I think he thought it would be funny and it was.

My tracksuit was way before any of that nonsense. Nobody was going to follow my fashion. Long socks would rectify this problem though. The top still fitted well, but the trousers were a definite look. There was also a faded stain on the bottom that had never quite come out... mmm nice. Even I knew its days were numbered, I just hoped mine were not.

There had been no sign of Scary Man and that worried me. It was like he was waiting for my track suit to be binned then he could get me. I had a bad feeling, a strange sensation that day as I put my tracksuit on that this might be the last time I put it on. I was convinced he would get me, it was only a matter of time. I was just making the most of it until that fateful day arrived. And that day was drawing closer. It had been too quiet for too long, and despite everyone saying he was long gone, I knew he wasn't. I just knew.

He was out there just waiting for his opportunity. I always felt he was playing tricks on me, just so I knew he was still around. The cobweb had been one of them, little things that only I would see. He was enjoying this, the stalk before the kill, the chase. He loved the fear in people's eyes, he got a kick out of it. That night on the road when he could have got me, he was laughing at me, with his head slowly turning towards me and his piercing eyes. It was all part of the game. That was about to come to an end, I knew it, any day now. I had a cold feeling. He was close. He had always been close but this time was different. Every door I opened I expected him to be standing there waiting. Every turn of my head I would think I saw him.

You don't imagine a feeling like that. it's your senses trying to warn you of impending danger. He was coming for me and I knew it. There is nothing you can do. If you hide under the bed, he will find you, and drag you out. Leaving the country wasn't an option, I didn't have a passport, let alone the funds to get me to remote Spain I only had seventy-eight pounds Freddie Laker Airlines was going to need more than that. Who wants to die under the bed, in a shit smelling tracksuit, whilst pissing themselves in to the bargain? Not me, I would take my chances in the woods. That was my best chance, the woods I knew so well, and I always had turbo mode, and if I had the Wheelie Pack in toe, I just might have a chance.

For now, we had the hut. That was my only hope. If Scary Man didn't know about it then he would never find me there. That would be my bolt hole when the shit hit the fan, and I knew it would. But I did worry about the flag, even though we had taken it down. It had lead us to the hut in the first place, maybe it had lead him there too, was that his plan. Even Dad and Mum didn't know about the hut, or that we were in the dark wood daily. As long as you were home for tea and did your chores, you were left to your own devices.

James had done his usual repairs to the hut. We had fitted a lock on the inside so we could lock ourselves in, and we had fitted a window with a grille on it so we could watch for intruders. We even had a small supply of food we had taken from the house just in case we had to bed in; Crisps, Wagon Wheels and emergency Fanta. The usual stuff, just like they would have had in the war. " Blitz 1941 an air raid shelter somewhere in London". *Mary I'm so sorry I just heard the news, how bad is it?* "Mary" *well my family home for five generations has gone, my husband, mother and father and all my six children are feared dead, and I am the last surviving member of*

THE GREEN TRACKSUIT

my family, I have nothing apart the clothes on my back, and I've laddered my fucking tights in to the bargain. I see Mary, Wagon Wheel? "Mary" oh that would be lovely George I don't suppose you would have a wee drop of Fanta to wash it down, oh that's much better.

We had bows and arrows, catapults and ball bearings. We even had an axe. I'm not sure what that was for, but we had it anyway. We thought it might come in handy. We had got more bushes and disguised the path up to the hut. You would never find it now.

Yes, we were feeling quite relaxed in the dark wood. Even Euan was comfortable wandering around the wood by himself. We just stayed clear of Maggie's Cottage. My advice, if you do stay next door to the devils House, would be- don't go there. It's the simple things that keep you alive, I like to think.

One day we were just about to leave, when we heard noises coming from Maggie's Cottage. Loud banging, smashing and screams. The looks on our faces as we all sat huddled in the Hut waiting for it to stop said it all, we were petrified. It sounded so close that we daren't leave. We didn't know what was out there. The door was locked and we sat and waited, just looking at one another, no words required. Euan looked like he was going to cry, I think we all wanted to cry. This was our worst nightmare. I fully expected the door to be pulled open at any time and we would be discovered. So, did James, I think - he had the axe in his hand.

Eventually the noise stopped, and we ventured out very cautiously at first. Whatever had been going on had stopped. It was still and silent again. Euan and Hector took to their heels and legged it back to ours for bikes then home, away from Maggie's. But Peter Easton and James said they were going to see what had been happening. I went with them. Why, I don't know.

The three of us carefully and quietly sneaked up to the back of the cottage from the Dark Wood. This took us directly in to the back garden. We lay there in the undergrowth, and slowly crawled forward until we could see the door. The little red door was open. Bloody hell, we had never seen it open. I didn't think it *could* open. We crept closer through the bushes, then we stopped and watched for about ten minutes, in complete silence. Our anxious looks were conversation enough.

Nothing moved. It was eerily silent. We moved closer. We were nearly at the back door. We stood up and moved forward, pushing our bodies tight against the cottage wall, and edged towards the open door, until we were right beside it. I've never been so scared as I was in that moment. I was trying to stop my body from shaking, but I couldn't. Was HE inside waiting for us?

Peter Easton quickly poked his head round the half open door. His eyes returned significantly larger than when they had left. He looked at us and uttered one word - Ready? This was the point when we should have stopped and gone home and told Mum and Dad. But we didn't. Peter Easton turned and walked in to the cottage, James followed, then me. Oh, my God. We walked in the door and went through another door, into a small dark room. The air was thick with dust. No one here. Then through another door into a small hall: nothing. We passed through a room with a range that must have been the kitchen, and back out the front door...and breathe!

We waited. The cottage was completely silent. No one was here, but we still waited, just to be sure. We looked at each other in disbelief at what we had seen. I had to go back. I walked back in the door, James and Peter Easton followed. This time I remembered to breathe. We walked slower this time, having established that no one was here. I still couldn't stop shaking. I'm not sure I can describe what lay in front of us. I thought I was going to pee myself if I hadn't done so already.

Every door to every room had a star on it, hand painted in red paint with what looked like a goat's head with horns in the middle. They were on the walls too. There was writing as well. Each room had something written on the wall in red paint. The living room above the fire had WE KNOW WHO YOU ARE AND WE ARE GOING TO KILL YOU, written in large writing in two lines across the wall, one above the other. The kitchen wall had similar, WE ARE GOING TO FIND YOU AND KILL YOU. There was more writing on the hall wall but I couldn't understand it. The place was a wreck, every door hanging off, the floor covered in glass and bits of furniture. Everything was broken and smashed. It was like walking in slow motion, every detail more horrible than the last.

We couldn't believe what we were seeing, that this was happening. Either Miss Mackenzie had redecorated, or this was a place of much evil. I suspected the latter. I went in and out three times, every time coming out to breathe. The air wasn't nice in there, so thick and dusty and so little of it. I was so shocked by what I was seeing, I was still shaking.

On closer examination, the lock on the front door had been broken, and the wood around it damaged. This door had been forced open. The one thing I couldn't understand was the kitchen table remained undamaged and in the centre of it was a bowl of white sugar in perfect condition; not a grain spilt anywhere on the table. Yet the rest of the cottage was completely wrecked. Everything that could be broken was broken.

This was completely bizarre, but it was getting dark, and I wasn't hanging around here waiting to find out what was going on. So, we left it as we found it and headed home.

'Do you think this has been the work of vandals then?' I asked James,

'Maybe, but who?' he replied.

True: we didn't really have vandals in the country, vandals tend to be discouraged if there's a bus trip and a two-mile walk/ hike to their latest target. We certainly had none that were capable of this. Rural vandals might draw a picture of a cow or maybe a combine harvester, or even a large willy, but not this. We'd never seen anything like this.

You didn't break stuff in the country. Someone always saw you who knew your parents and you'd be busted, so you didn't bother. There was a respect for other people's property, but this, this was something else. We headed home and decided not to tell anyone what we had seen, which was a mistake. We weren't supposed to be over there anyway, and we would end up getting the blame. We decided to say nothing. We would go back tomorrow, when the light was better, and search for clues.

THE CURSE

I couldn't help but think this was the work of Scary Man. He had been seen there and then there was the beheaded fox incident. It seemed hard not to connect them. Fud! This was serious shit now. The house was wrecked. Miss Mackenzie was not going to be happy, and soon people were going to find out.

We returned home and said nothing, but thought of nothing else, James and I had a few knowing glances over out of date tea. I didn't sleep well if at all.

The next morning, Peter Easton arrived. We were going back to see what we would be confronted with today. Euan and Hector didn't turn up; we never expected them to. It was just the three of us. This was the days before mobile phones, so if you didn't turn up at the arranged time that was it. I had a few dates in later years that turned out like that. I thought she said meet me at eleven, which I did think was rather late. Turns out she said seven... she could have waited!

We did have a land line in the house, but it was in the kitchen and everybody or at least somebody would hear your conversation, some of you won't know what a landline is. It never went flat.

'Hi Euan/Hector, just wondered if you were coming over today? Maggie's cottage has been completely wrecked and the Scary Man who has been trying to kill me might be involved you coming?' That wasn't going to work.

Despite the fact it was a lovely day with brilliant sunshine, the cottage looked as dark as ever when we arrived. The door was still open and nothing looked to have changed. Still, we took our time and entered very cautiously just to be on the safe side.

I hated this house. It was an awful place. If this place had never existed that summer would have been much calmer, and my track suit would have smelled much better as well. But this horrible cottage with all its darkness and mystery had also made my summer in some sort of a sadistic way. As much as I hated it, I couldn't help but be drawn to it. There was too much unexplained weirdness surrounding it. Something kept making me go back there. Maybe that was the intention to lure you there.

It wasn't a normal cottage. Everyone knew that, and when

you're nine that's like a red rag to a bull. The fact we had been banned from going there also made it more of a temptation to go. It's like being told;

'Whatever you do: don't press that big red button!'
'Oops sorry, I had to press it...'
'Now the plane has no fuel... sorry.'

God, it looked even worse today. We did a quick round the rooms to check no one was there. It was clear. Still with only one door in and out, you were always conscious that if someone came in you were trapped and had no escape. One eye was always kept on the door. I would stand just inside the door and keep look out. Directly in front of me on the door to what had been the kitchen was a star shape, with a horned man in the centre. This was no star of Bethlehem. You wouldn't put this on top of your Christmas tree. Someone had taken great care drawing this. It looked awful, and despite wanting to ignore it, I couldn't help but look at it. I can only assume the horned face in the centre was the devil.

At the time, I didn't know what this was, but I knew it wasn't good. I've since found out it was a five-pointed Satanic Star and a symbol of Devil worship. So that's nice.

There were several of them throughout the house, about six in total and mainly on doors. They were horrible looking things. To this day, I've never seen anything quite as disturbing as those bloody stars. James came and took over watch so I could go in for a better look... oh great. This wasn't a good place to be and despite my better judgement I went in. My heart was racing and I was forgetting to breathe again. There was a stale damp smell in the air, and where the shafts of sunlight illuminated the room you could see the thick dusty air hanging. No wonder I could hardly breathe.

It was as horrible as I remembered. With every step, something would crack or break under your foot, glass and china covered the floor. You couldn't walk quietly, that was for sure. There were six stars in total, all the same, meticulously drawn in red paint that had run, just to make it scarier. There were three different pieces of writing. We referred to them as The Curses... well, you would. They all appeared to be warnings or threats. The first one in the front room said, WE KNOW WHO YOU ARE AND WE ARE GOING TO KILL YOU. Each letter was about six inches high in red paint. It doesn't get much more threatening than that. The second in the kitchen said WE ARE GOING TO FIND YOU, and the third which looked like it hadn't been finished and was harder to read said, STAY AWAY IF YOU KNOW WHATS GOOD FOR YOU. Bit late for that now: I'm standing in front of it reading it.

That was all the writing and symbols. Everything else was broken and smashed. Nobody had been staying here in a while. The wallpaper was coming off and the walls were all damp. It had been empty until this had been done to it. You couldn't stay in there for long. It was horrible and breathing was uncomfortable, or maybe I was just in such a panic I was forgetting to breathe. It was an assault on the senses being in there.

We had been in here too long. We were just heading out the door when Peter Easton found hidden behind a door, a very small narrow staircase that lead upstairs. It was rotten and a lot of the steps were broken. So, there was an upstairs. That explained the windows I had seen on the front; so small you could hardly see them. Peter put his foot on the first step and it snapped in two. The wood was really rotten. This would have to wait for another visit. Nobody was going up or down these steps. We had never considered there might be an upstairs. It looked dark and grim, and we were all happy not to have to go there for now.

I had seen a similar door in the kitchen. I went to check, just in case there was another set of steps leading somewhere else. It was just a cupboard with another bowl of sugar in it. I glanced to the table. The sugar bowl had gone. Who moved the sugar? Who moved the bloody sugar? Shit! Time to go, go, go!

I know what you're thinking, why? Why go to this cottage when you know it's a bad place? We have clearly established that it was a very bad place. The thing is, you need to know, and once you find out a little, you need to know the rest. You need to know the end, you need to know that good will prevail over evil, otherwise we are all stuffed. So, as much as I wanted to stay away I couldn't, I just couldn't. I had to find out. Yes, it was an adrenaline rush, but it went way beyond rush. It was like a heart attack. I would have been much happier going to a Roller Disco to get my thrills.

Town dwellers always used to ask me, is it scary living in the country? 'Townser's', who had street lights, and buses, and more than one shop, probably within walking distance. 'YES! It is.' I always used to reply. But there's less chance you will get killed by some psychopathic killer running through the streets, randomly killing strangers, before throwing himself in front of the Heinz baked bean lorry. You just don't get that in the country. But if there is a knock at the door in the middle of the night, and you are confronted by some crystal meth, knife wielding maniac, you know they've come for you. It's not a mistake! They weren't out for a walk and stumbled across your house by accident, and fancied a spot of random murdering before tea, NO! They came for YOU.

Staying in the country, was definitely safer. It may have appeared scary, but generally you were pretty safe. Staying in a town or a city, you had crime and were much more aware of it, and had to be. In the country, you could forget about all that. Your biggest danger was staying on a farm; chickens with guns, nails sticking up out of the ground, farm machinery, Mum's cooking. These were the real threats. But if trouble did come to your door step, you couldn't ignore it. It's much more obvious, when there's little else going on. So, as much as I thought this could properly damage me, mentally and physically, I had to keep looking. I had to find him and find out why he had come for me. Fud

The sugar bowl had moved overnight, from the kitchen table to the cupboard. When we had left the previous day the sugar bowl had been on the table, of that I'm one hundred percent sure. It was the last thing I saw. Peter Easton and James said they hadn't moved it. I knew they hadn't. Yet on our return it was in a cupboard. Some else had moved it, someone else had been there, someone else knew what had happened to Maggie's.

We decided to watch the cottage for a few days and see who was going there. In the field in front of Maggie's, the field where Sharn boy had been born, there was a large pile of stones. It was at the bottom of the field, far enough away and open enough to see

THE CURSE

anyone coming, so we made base camp there. Our heads like meerkats bobbing up and down from behind our pile of rocks. For two days, we watched... nothing. Obviously, night time was unmonitored, but for two days we saw nothing come or go.

We set some of our usual cunning traps, just in case they were coming at night or in from the Dark Wood side. The usual things; twigs and stones against doors, door opens, it moves...basic stuff. After our three-day surveillance, we returned to check the traps. There was no need to. Before we were anywhere near the door, we could see where it had been open, it was now closed.

FLOATY MAN

By now it was clearly apparent that someone else was going to the cottage regularly: the sugar bowl and the traps had proved that. And yet, we knew that the police had not been informed that the cottage had been broken into. So, either the person that had been going there had been the one who had broken in, or they had found it open and were using it. We always assumed that the stars and writing had been done by the vandals, but what if they had already been there and the vandals had just smashed the place up? Maybe the devil worship stuff had been the reason it got smashed up? None of it made any sense. It was definitely another 'Cheesy Fud' scenario.

For us, the stars and the writing were the problem. Yes, we knew that people did break in to places, to steal things, but they didn't cover the walls in satanic symbols and slogans. We didn't know anything about Devil Worship and we didn't know anyone who did. Apart from Peter Easton's babysitter of course, but clearly, she hadn't done this. She would be too busy eating biscuits and scaring kids on another babysitting job I suspect. I think bad stuff had been going on here for a while, and the break in had just given us the opportunity to see inside the cottage. Maybe it had been like this all along.

That would explain all the stories and strange goings on. It couldn't just be a coincidence. It didn't explain where Miss Mackenzie was. I know I thought she was a witch, but that was only because of how she dressed and looked, I never really thought she actually was. I still found it very hard to believe, that little old lady was worshiping the devil in a little cottage in the woods, here of all

FLOATY MAN

places. I had my doubts.

There was another option: this was a trap to lure us to the cottage. We had been in the hut the day when we heard all the noises, then we came to look. Maybe that was the intention? To get us here, so we could see the writing on the walls which had been predicted by the Ouija board. The red scrawls on the cottage walls were curses, and the board had spelt curse: that was unexplainable. I couldn't even think about that. To believe it would have been to believe that the Ouija board had worked, and surely that wasn't possible? Even if it had been varnished twice.

No, it was an elaborate masterplan James had hatched to get rid of his much cuter younger brother. It had been years in the planning: he could no longer take my beauty and charm. I was destined for greatness and he knew it. He must stop me, before I took over the world and created an army of green tracksuit -wearing bottom-flashing lunatics. It would have explained all the electrocuting. As we speak he is probably sitting in his lair, a hollowed-out volcano, stroking his bald Chihuahua, Mrs Alotta Barking, before putting the finishing touches to his new laser in a vain bid to end me, once and for all.

No, James was taking this far too seriously to be involved. He was even suggesting that we get the guns from the house. We had several guns and yes, we probably could have taken them, but if anything had happened us and Dad could have ended up in really serious trouble. If you have a gun and someone jumps out in front of you, it's all too easy to shoot them. Then you find out it was Miss Mackenzie hanging out her washing and you've just blown her away, because she waved a bed sheet in your face.

'Sorry, Miss M. That sheet's going to need another wash now, and there's a hole in it...oh and you might be dead'

No guns for now. We knew where they were if we needed them. Hopefully we wouldn't need them and this would all go away and I could return to picking flowers in the meadow and riding my girls bike. Please.

One day soon the Policeman would come back, and that would blow the whole thing wide open. Then a swarm of Police would descend, and there would be multiple arrests. Helicopters, and the whole area would be cordoned off, while they carried out forensic tests. We would be hailed as heroes, protectors of the countryside, single handily we had saved the whole community for certain murder, three cheers for Peter and the wheelie pack, hip hip hooray. Of course, this did all depend on the Policeman coming back, and there were no guarantees he would. He probably had more pressing issues, like a cow on the road, or an angry escaped goat on the loose, eating the flowers in Mrs Fraser's garden.

She had a lovely garden, and if she treated the goat anything like she treated us when she caught us stealing her plums, then that goat was in for a stern aristocratic bollocking from a Tartan trouser suit-wearing Janette Krankie lookalike. Enjoy those shrubs, Mr Gruff: they will be your last. No one messes with Jannette's bush and lives.

'Hello, is that the police? This is Mrs Fraser at 4 Teelig Cottage. Dispatch a constable at once! My bush is being mauled, hurry! 'That is probably a conversation that has actually happened.

So far, the adults had been useless: too busy with grownup issues to have time for our devil worship dilemma in the woods. So, the Wheelie Pack, (well, what was left of it, which was three; sometimes Hector showed up. Euan was still hiding in a wardrobe somewhere,) took the executive decision, to write a letter to said devil worshipper arranging to meet them. We would leave it in the cottage, for whoever was staying there. It was a completely bonkers idea.

'Dear Devil worshipper, hope you're well? We just wondered if you were looking for any human sacrifices, and if so we would love to help…yours sincerely stupid boys, Aka dinner.

Yes. Completely Bonkers. But that's what we did. We wrote a letter saying we would like to meet them, and we would return the following day to make formal introductions. I don't know why, but this seemed the logical thing to do. We were out of ideas, so the next thing was to make contact. We wrote the letter, on Mum's best lavender-scented writing paper. Well, we wanted to make a good impression- less chance of death, or being put in a pot with some carrots.

James did the writing in large blocked capitals. We put it in an envelope, then James burnt it slightly over a candle, just to make it look old. I don't know why. We were in unchartered waters here, and maybe an old dirty slightly singed lavender scented letter would be more appealing to the Dark Side? We all set off to hand deliver the letter to Maggie's. Even Hector was back, he had not seen the cottage from the inside yet, he was in for a treat. I could see some bed wetting times ahead for Hector.

We arrived at the cottage. The door was closed. We waited and watched for a while. All seemed calm. Eventually we all edged forward and Peter Easton tried the door. It was open. Tentatively, we opened the door and waited. Nothing. There appeared to be no one home, thank God.

We all crept in. Peter kept watch at the door. It was as miserable as ever. Hector was speechless, or he just couldn't breathe. It looked the same as we had come to remember it. This was not a good place, this was a troubled house, and as soon as you walked in the door you could feel it. To this day, the thought of that place sends shivers down my spine, even writing about it sends shivers through me. The most scared I've ever been was in that house, and I will never go anywhere near it as long as I live. And to this day I never have.

James quickly placed the letter on top of the fire place. In this ghastly place, it didn't look out of place, all dirty and burnt. Our ageing process had worked a treat. any self-respecting devil worshiper would be lucky to receive such a lovely letter.

'Right, let's get out of here.'

We headed back to ours. We would return the next day at six o clock, as the letter said. Then we would meet whoever was staying there. If it was my friend from the road Scary Man, we were about to find out, and if he was evil, we were about to find out. This was a big moment.

Had we just imagined it all? Was Scary Man just a gypsy after all, wandering about our woods at night? Had the writing and satanic symbols just been the work of kids, who were good at drawing, maybe studying art at the university, out for a walk? Who knows Mr Fox might have been involved in a tragic traffic accident and they just found him and hung him up for a bit before burying him? We were about to find out.

I knew if it was Scary Man staying there, he would come. Anyone else would want to keep their identity secret and would probably not turn up, but Scary would show. Everyone had their own theory on who, if anyone, would be there. Hector had thought the whole letter idea had been a mistake, and we should stay away. We probably should have. Peter Easton was taking it seriously, I think, but he always seemed to think it was all a bit of fun too. He predicted no one would turn up, but he was coming along, of course, just in case there was any punching to be done. He was our main weapon so this was good news.

Trigger happy James still thought we should have guns as we didn't know how many of them there might be. Yes, this may be life threatening, James, but I'm not being the one with a gun, doing the threatening. No guns James- down boy! James was expecting more than one person to be there. I'd not thought of that: for me there was only one person who would show up- Scary Man.

It was a Friday, like any other day. The clouds looked the same, the air smelt the same, but this was no ordinary Friday. I made sure to put on my tracksuit that morning, long socks to negotiate the gap between ankles and trousers and my very best running shoes. Well, I only had one pair, they would do. The Wheelie Pack formed around lunchtime and waited. The full squad, even Euan was there. Well done Euan. Five of us- that was a good number. Surely one of us could get away and raise the alarm if it all went pear shaped?

We set off for our arranged meeting. We had sticks and a catapult and some ball bearings. God, it sounds like David and Goliath! It was a nice day; the sun was out and bright. We made our way through the dark woods, stopping at the hut for the axe. Ok, you can bring the axe but no guns, we told James. The wood was calm and still. Even the Dark Wood seemed unusually pleasant today.

As we neared the cottage, we grew more tense. We were early, but couldn't contain ourselves any longer and had set off anyway, arriving half an hour earlier than we had said we would. This would give us time to scope the place out, and see if we saw anyone arriving. This was the point that Euan said he would have to go on the grounds that he was crapping himself. Well, he had done well to get this far and I fully expected this to happen.

Just the four of us then. We sat at the edge of the dark wood and watched, carefully examining the building for any signs of movement. It was just before six, maybe about ten to, when we moved forward to the door. Hector was to stay at the door and keep watch, the rest of us were to go in. Peter Easton went first. He tried the door. It was open. He opened it wide with a bang hoping to startle anyone that might have been in there: nothing.

The three of us went in very slowly, leaving Hector at the door to keep watch. sticks at the ready. James with his axe, like the woodsman in Little Red Riding Hood off to kill the wolf.

'What big ears you have, Peter!'

'I've always had big ears James. Down, boy!'

We were in and the cottage appeared to be empty. No one was here and the letter was still sitting on the fire place. James checked it. It was still sealed. It had not been opened. There would be no one coming today. We were all slightly disappointed, relieved but disappointed. We were all pumped up for a showdown and the letter hadn't even been opened. We would leave it where it was and try again tomorrow.

James suggested we explore upstairs. We'd never been up there before, and this seemed as good at time as any. Hector came off lookout duty, and we closed the door. We all attempted to climb the rotting staircase. Every step either completely snapped, or cracked as soon as you put any weight on it. Using our sticks as supports we managed to negotiate the stairs, without anyone breaking a leg, which was an achievement. After some time, all four of us were upstairs.

There were two tiny rooms with nothing in them, just some straw for insulation. It was very dark. The two small windows on the front were broken, but let in only a little light. If downstairs was creepy, this was worse. It's' bare stark darkness was completely haunting. The house was silent. James picked up a large piece of wood to see if there was anything behind it. We all watched. There wasn't, just a book. Jamie picked it up and looked at it, then he dropped it. We could all see the red writing on the front THE SATANIC RITUALS, companion to the satanic bible We all stood in silence just looking at it. Crikey, I didn't like this.

Just then we heard the front door being pushed open. We froze to the spot, then we heard footsteps come in the door and stop. Nobody moved, or breathed. We stood completely motionless. The footsteps moved through to the front room. We all looked at one another with total fear in our eyes. We were trapped upstairs, and if whoever was downstairs opened that letter they would know we were here.

There was no way we could get out. It had been hard enough coming up the stairs. You couldn't run down those stairs, four of us, before they walked the five feet to the bottom of the stairs. We would be caught for sure. We heard the letter being opened. There was a pause. I looked round the faces. How nobody screamed and ran down or fell down those bloody stairs I will never know. Complete fear and strain on everybody's face, yet perfectly still. How long could we keep this up for? Four people trapped upstairs in a room with the Devils Bible lying on the floor, and a potential lunatic downstairs, about to realise we were upstairs.

We remained remarkably composed, it was complete fear. I've never been so scared in my life. We had no way out. Several minutes passed without any movement from downstairs. As though they were listening for any sound. We made none, but not moving was becoming increasingly difficult. Silence. We waited, then we heard the steps again, moving back towards the door, heavy boots that clonked like wood on wood. I'd heard them before.

They stopped.

'Please go, please just close the door and go!'

Then I heard a sound I will never forget, as long as I live. What happened next is as fresh in my memory as if it was happening now. A boot hit the first step of the stairs. We heard it crack and then the second step. He was coming up the stairs.

In disbelief at what was happening we remained motionless. Then James ran to the window and started smashing the remaining glass, Peter Easton started doing the same at the window in front of him. The silence was broken, and utter panic set in. We could hear the steps crashing and breaking behind us.

Hector squeezed himself out the small window, James grabbed and pushed me forward out the other window. I was now perched on a rusty corrugated iron roof, about fifteen feet from the ground, the roof was old and rusty, what the fud do I do know. I jumped and just cleared the barbed wire fence outside. I lay on the ground and looked up. I could see James and Peter Easton climbing out the windows and jumping. How we got out those tiny windows I will never know. We basically forced ourselves out. We were up and on our feet and running flat out. All our thoughts of sticks and catapults protecting us had gone. Peter Easton was out in front. He was supposed to be our main weapon.

I had gone from lying on the ground straight in to turbo mode. My legs were running before I had even got up. Everyone was in turbo mode. I've never run so fast in my life. Peter Easton was heading for the bottom of the field to the large pile of stones we had used for our surveillance. We all followed. I was now in last place and despite the fact I was exhausted, I was still increasing my speed. We all reached the stone pile and slid behind it.

He had come, at exactly six o clock. How had he known? The letter hadn't been opened. It was definitely Scary Man. I'd recognise those boots anywhere, and he had been coming up those stairs at speed, that was for sure. If those stairs hadn't been rotten we would have been caught. My leg was bleeding, so was James's hand. Peter Easton's as well. We lay behind the rock pile gasping for breath. No one dared look back up to the cottage. James eventually popped his head up to look.

Then he stood up, we all did. Why had he stood up? We will be seen, you tit!

I looked back up to the cottage. There were three people coming directly towards us from the cottage. They were about one hundred yards away. They were half way down the bloody field. How the hell did they get there and so quickly? They were moving really fast. We had come down that field in seconds and they were right there behind us. We were fit, really fit. We lived on an athlete's diet. There are only a few people in the world that could have covered that ground in that time. What the fud was going on?

Directly in the middle was the man I had met on the road that night, Scary Man. I'd recognise him in the street today, forty years on. On either side of him were two women dressed in long black dresses. Where the bloody hell had they come from? They both had long jet-black hair and thin pale white faces. Where the fuddy hell had they come from? They were nearly on us. What was going on?

"He's floating" said Hector,

WHAT? I looked, then I looked again, then I looked at James and Peter Easton. The blood had literally drained from their faces. He was floating, his legs weren't moving, neither were his arms apart from one that was gesturing towards us to come to him. Everyone stood motionless like we had just done in the loft, but for a different reason, this time, disbelief. He was nearly on us, but we couldn't stop looking. There was a man floating towards us at speed, another ten seconds and he would be on us and still nobody could stop looking,

James put up the familiar cry, RUN! I turn and ignited like a rocket, fully expecting his hand on my shoulder at any moment. I could almost feel his breath on my back. He was that close, inches from grabbing me, and he was clearly going for me. I engaged every mode I've ever had, the same mode I had engaged that night on the road, crazy mode, out of control running that only gets faster, the further you go, nitrous running. I wasn't even sure I could out run him. He was right behind me.

'What about chasing some of the rest of them? Bugger off!'

He was shouting 'Come here, boys,' in a very strange voice. He was about four feet behind me. One wrong step, and I was caught, one foot not positioned perfectly and I was done for. I turned to check the distance again. I could see his face clearly now, too clearly. His teeth were rotten and his thin pale face stared directly at me. He grinned slightly, through his long wispy grey beard. This was it, his hand was inches from my back.

I couldn't run any faster. It was time to concede defeat and stop and face the music. I was done. I turned to see where the boys were. They were just about at the path. We had been running to the corner of the field. There was a path there that at ran adjacent to a wall and along the side of another field. The path was narrow, with lots of low hanging branches. He would have to slow down there. If I could just make it there, I might have a chance.

But I had been running at full pelt, flat out for 4-5 minutes, I had nothing left, absolutely nothing, and I was slowing. I was ten feet from the path. I could hear James shouting 'Run, Peter, RUN! Just then Scary grabbed me on the back of my tracksuit. he had touched me, he had actually touched me His hand tightened on the cloth. He was starting to pull me back. oh my god this was it His grip was tightening, I saw James stop, then Peter Easton, Hector kept running, cheers Hector. I couldn't shake his hand off me, I pulled and shrugged but I couldn't shake his hand from me. I was caught and done for, unless, in one last attempt to break free I pushed both my arms behind me and ran forward. My tracksuit top slid off my back, along with his hand. I was free, it had worked I ran and reached the path. James and Peter Easton pushed me forward and we all set off running again. Holy shit that was close.

Floating. Yes, I know, it's hard to believe, and I can't really explain it if I'm honest, but he was floating. His legs weren't moving. I realise this is a difficult thing to believe, and I have spent many years trying to process this. I still can't find a logical reason, even today's technology is not advanced enough for someone to be able to do that. But I can't say anything else other than he was floating, just above the ground. His boots looked like they were on the ground, but when he moved his feet didn't, and he went forward at speed. That's as much as I can say.

I was there I saw it and so did James, Hector and Peter Easton. None of us were in any doubt as to what we saw. As hard as it was to believe, he was floating, and even today James and I still refer to him as Floaty Man.

THE GREEN TRACKSUIT

Of all the strangeness this story entails, curses and satanic pentangles, encounters on the road at night, foxes with no heads, it is this that troubles me the most. I can rationalise the rest, put it down to something else, find another reason for its happening. But this I saw, in front of me and as much as I knew it was not possible, I saw it never the less. One pair of eyes could make a mistake, be confused in the sunlight, but four pairs of eyes, all saying and seeing the same thing is hard to ignore. To believe something is impossible is one thing, to see it actually happen in front of you is quite another.

I don't expect you to believe me. I wouldn't, in your shoes, but I can only tell you what I saw, and I remain as convinced today as I did then, he was floating ...

We tore down the small path in pairs side by side, Peter Easton and Hector still in front. Peter Easton the puncher was doing a lot of running, for a tough guy, but this went way beyond, standard violence. What happens if you punch a floating man? We were not about to find out.

I think there was stark realisation that we were in completely over our heads, and were in real danger. Up until now it had all been substantial evidence, nothing had happened. But now we were being chased, at speed by a potential mad man. Well, he was definitely mad, the shouting had conveyed that. This was no longer a game, this was now a chase, and God knows what he was going to do to us if he did catch us. I wasn't feeling positive about it, to say the least.

The branches across the path were really low. We were ducking and jumping over the low ones. I looked across to James. He had gone, he had stopped. I stopped.

'He's not following us,' said James.

I couldn't actually speak, I was more likely to throw up. I was on my knees, and gasping for air.

'What the Fud is going on James?' I blurted out. 'HE WAS FLOATING... FLOATING!'

James looked worried, really worried, not his usual inventing face like he was just about to attempt to turn an old washing machine in to a Jetpack. No not that face. I hadn't seen this face before and I didn't like it.

'Get up!' said James. 'Get up now!'

'What?'

'He's still coming!' said James.

I was still on my knees, and still trying to catch my breath. My arm was bleeding. It was not a deep cut, but there was still a lot of blood. Peter Easton and Hector were now half way down the corn field that was the other side of the path, heading to the road beside the quarry, they had also stopped.

We were used to being chased. This wasn't our first time. Our quarry adventures had resulted in being chased on several occasions. These chases never usually lasted very long. We were fit and fast and our chasers were generally adults and would give up pretty quickly. This time was different. This time, he was still coming.

'Get up!' said James. 'He's coming up behind us.'

He had gone further along and up an old road and was now a few hundred yards behind us. We would head to the quarry. It was big and we could lose him there. We couldn't go home. As much as I wanted to go home, I wasn't bringing him with us.

We started running again across the field to where the boys were. By this point, they had seen he was still behind us and had started running again. Scary was nearly in the field. Why am I always last? I thought 'For once can I not be last? Not today.'

I had got a second wind and had caught up with the rest of the pack. We were out of the field and heading along the road towards the back of the quarry. He was still coming and still appeared to be floating. Everyone was in a panic. Hector kept saying 'he is a ghost!'. He was quite hysterical and clearly not coping very well. None of us were, but we had to keep moving. We started to climb the hill up to the back of the quarry. Hector said he was going to stay on the road and keep running. If he went across the fields he would eventually get home although it was a good two miles. There was no time to think. We headed up the hill and Hector kept going.

THE GREEN TRACKSUIT

It was a steep climb up to the top of the quarry but we had done it many times. You had to be careful when you got to the top, because it was a hundred and fifty feet drop to the bottom and certain death if you went over there. We slowed down. There was no fence round the top and it would have been all too easy to walk off the edge. We stopped close to the top. We would see him coming from here and we were knackered.

'What was that?' said Peter Easton.

James wasn't listening he was too busy watching to see if he was still coming.

'He was floating.' I said.

Peter Easton looked at me and said, "How is that possible? He was moving so fast.'

'Are you ok?' Peter asked me.

'No,' I said, 'he nearly got me.'

'I thought he had.' Peter said.

'I think he has stopped.' said James. 'I can't see him coming.'

The three of us sat down behind some bushes, although James was still keeping an eye out. Nobody said anything. Our faces were beetroot red from all the running. None of us could believe what had just happened. He had been so close to catching me, and I no longer had my tracksuit top now to prove it. He had grabbed me, god knows what he was going to do to me, but he had actually touched me, why me.

We were about ten feet from the edge of the quarry. We appeared to have lost him, but we were all still in a state of shock. After ten minutes of catching our breath, we decided it was time to move. We would head down the side of the quarry towards the dynamite shed, in the opposite direction from where we had been chased by Floaty Man. We stood up and started walking. My leg was sore and bleeding. I looked down at it, and when I looked back up, coming straight towards me was Floaty Man,

I couldn't get out of the way. He pushed me and I fell backwards. I felt like I was falling forever. I thought I had gone over the side of the quarry, but I had landed perilously close to the edge. James pulled me back to my feet and pushed me forward. I

FLOATY MAN

saw Peter Easton pick up a rock and throw it at him. I didn't see if it hit him, but I heard a dull thump and a horrible shriek. I was struggling to run my leg was so sore. Peter Easton and James dragged me down the side of the quarry at full speed. We passed the dynamite shed and headed straight for home. We needed help. We never looked back we just kept running as fast as we could straight up the hill to ours, the boys dragging me most of the way, I thought I was going to die that day, and when he pushed me I thought I had, I couldn't believe it we couldn't believe it. Peter Easton had thrown a big massive rock, it was the first one he could see and big, that must have hurt, and that noise, I will never forget that, not of this earth.

James said he was getting the rifle. When we arrived home we all ran straight in to the house. James went and got the gun, I went to tell Dad. The house was empty. No one was home. Oh, for God sake! James loaded the gun and we went outside, climbed on top of the porch roof and waited. We lay there for three hours, James with the gun ready. He never came, just as well because we bloody would have shot him.

We were petrified sitting on that roof with a two two rifle, fully loaded, we would have shot anything that came up the road, lucky nothing did, we patched ourselves up with some of mum's plasters and bandages. How I wasn't dead I didn't know, I thought he would come again that night for sure.

We decided not to tell Dad and Mum after all. It would lead them to Maggie's, and we would get the blame for everything. So, we said nothing. We wanted to but I was scared Dad would go after him and get hurt, this was no normal person. So, nothing was said.

We were different boys after that day, never far from home and I was never far from Dads side. James slept with a rifle under his bed from then on. He never came for me that night, but one of these nights he will, I know it.

SUMMERS END

Lying washed and folded on my bed was my school uniform. I say mine, but of course it had been James's before me. Some things never change. Still, at least it didn't have tights with it. Mum had sent me to school wearing two pairs of tights before. Yes, it might have been a cold day, but really. I'm a modern thinking type of guy, but two pairs of ten denier tights under your trousers is a stretch, literally, even for me.

If anything had happened and my trouser leg had ridden up at school, I would have been in serious trouble. Can you imagine getting caught at school wearing tights? And not just tights, but your Mums tights and two pairs of them. I took great care that day at School, and only went to the toilet when I knew I was alone, you didn't want someone walking in and catch you at the urinal with your tights half down. I even took care walking home, I didn't want to get hit by a car and rushed to hospital.

Doctor: 'Nine-year-old Caucasian male, car crash.'

Nurse: "Doctor, he appears to be wearing tights. Two pairs actually.'

Doctor "Really? My god! It's worse than I thought.'

Although I must say my legs did feel amazing. but where does it end…stockings? No, I wasn't doing that again. Mum had caught me off guard that day and before I knew I was out the door in tights. Never again! Well...never is a long time... .NO, Peter, NO MORE TIGHTS!

I was stronger now, well I'm not sure, I was, I spent most of my time petrified if I'm honest, but eventually that fades and is replaced with an arrogance for life, if you're coming for me come, I don't care anymore, come on then, so far, he hasn't, but I still keep looking over my shoulder. Why me I will never know, well I say never, I'm not that sure. We never saw Floaty Man again. We went back to the hut a few weeks later, but only to get some stuff we had left there. Someone had been there. Our traps had all moved. I suspect Floaty Man had gone there looking for us. I think the hut had been part of his plan, and we nearly fell for it. We never went back to the hut after that. We went and recovered the top of my tracksuit, which I picked up and carried home on a stick and put in the washing basket, I wasn't touching that till it had been washed, it was fine if mum did though. We stayed well clear of Maggie's. We never went back there again either. After that we stayed out of the Dark Wood completely. Stay out of the dark wood that's my advice.

Mrs Mackenzie had apparently gone to stay with her sister. Turns out her sister was alive after all, which would make her better company for Mrs Mackenzie. The Policeman never did come back. Typical! No one ever seemed to find out about the vandalism. A few years later the house was sold and pulled down and a new house built on the same spot. Bugger that! I wouldn't be building a house there! Of course, they didn't know what we knew.

Mary from the Spar and I married in the fall of eighty-six, and remain together... I joke, we did stay friends. Duncan from the Ironmongers, continues to squeeze himself in to a younger man's clothes, and is still the Mr Lover Lover of the Highlands. And Dr Fergusson became a better Doctor, after I had introduced him to pain, and we always had a knowing drum stick nod for each other after that.

The Wheelie Pack had experienced something that would see them friends for life. It was like we had survived a plane crash and for many years we remained inseparable. Although I don't know where any of them are now.

Except for James: I know where he is. In fact, he's upstairs in the loft doing a spot of wiring for me. I hope that works out ok?

TODAY 2017: THE BIRCHES.

Dad's Castle lies on its own, empty and dark, not quite a ruin, but not fit for much else. What had once been our home is now just bits of wood and crumbling stone, and a very over grown garden. No crazy children to be heard. Our fortress, no longer Mums pickling emporium, is failing and falling. The laughter has faded, the music has stopped, the screaming children have grown up, and Dad's zoo has closed its gates. Day by day, the Highlands gradually reclaims what was rightfully Hers all along.

Dad had built this home with his own hands and I loved every nail that built it, every grain in every bit of wood. There's barely a tree there I hadn't climbed, fallen out of, or carved, my name in. This wasn't a house, this was a home. Sweat and tears might have built it, but it was love and laughter that filled it. One man's dream had changed the lives of all who lived there, none more so than his children's. We were part of a fantastic journey, and lucky to have had such a great man that we could call Dad.

He made our childhood the most magical adventure any child would want, and filled it with fun and laughter. You never knew what he was going to do next, and I loved him for that. Every power cut, snow storm, fallen tree, fire, flood: he made them all fun. He was such a loved man and by so many, none more so than me. I cry as I write this.

Dad would die at the Birches, aged sixty-eight, in the countryside he loved so much. The place where he had built his dream, and where he made all our dreams come true. The only disadvantage of having such an amazing Dad is that your world falls apart when he is no longer in it. The family shattered in to

TODAY 2017: THE BIRCHES

pieces. Dad was the glue and without him we were lost and still are.

Mum would follow him a few years later. Like us, lost without her beloved Tom. Without our parents, the world is a bit darker, the hills a bit steeper and the roads a lot longer. But we take comfort in having lived in a time and space where we could be free, and for a while were part of the most amazing family.

It was Dad and Mum's home for over forty years, a Tetris of buildings perched on top of a hill, in the middle of nowhere, surrounded by the beautiful Highland countryside. In winter, it would put any Christmas card to shame. You could wake up to fresh snow and deer in your front field. In summer, it was a million different shades of vibrant green.

There was a silence that only existed there, apart from the odd roaring lion, or the distant sound of the drums being played badly.

Even when it was just Mum and Dad and they should have sold up and got somewhere smaller in the village, they couldn't. They loved the place too much. I think it was all the fun and happy memories they had there. They couldn't leave.

Mum would eventually move to the village, but only after Dad had passed away, too young, and too soon. The Birches lost it laughter after that. Mum struggled on for a few years, she literally had to be dragged away in the end.

Growing up in the country is something that never leaves you. Of course, you can and probably will leave the country life, but it will never leave you. There's something about being part of the changing scenery, the ever-changing wildlife and the silence and the solitude that makes you notice more. Every day you see or hear something different, and you engage more with your surroundings. It's not man made. It's a living growing thing and your part of it and always will be. no matter where you go or what you do with your life You will always have a longing to go back there.

Hopefully this story made you laugh, and remember a more care free time, when we were all children, when we were free. For me, it was journey back in time to the place where I was born, where I grew up, and to a place I loved. In a landscape that was unique, untouched and every now and again simply stunning. That's part of my genetic makeup now, the countryside, the Highlands. It shaped who I am, the things I do today. I learnt from my time there. What I learned is not always useful but it's always there just in case you need to abseil down a wall at short notice.

Floaty Man was real, and even now, I stay out of the shadows. I still look over my shoulder, expecting to see him there, following me. Sometimes I think it's only a matter of time, my luck will run out one day, and he will catch me.

But, for now, I'm off to buy a suitably ridiculous tweed suit in the hope I might continue my father's good work. While I can, I already have the red socks.

Stay out of the shadows, stay in the light, beware of the darkness. He's still out there, waiting for me, and for you. Statistics show that less than one percent of the population will be affected by Devil worship in their lifetime so you have nothing to worry about.

Except I was walking home from the station the other day, and I heard this noise, the sound of what might have been wooden heels, behind me, clonking on the road. I turned and thought I saw someone turn away from me, and walk off back up the hill.

Someone I'd known all my life.

#0202 - 200818 - C0 - 234/156/6 - PB - DID2280434